I0762743

TO

____

FROM

____

DATE

____

EMBRACE YOUR NEW

Discovering God's
Restorative Power

MELISSA HORVATH

First Edition, August 2025

Published by:

21154 Highway 16 East
Siloam Springs, AR 72761
dayspring.com

Written By: Melissa Horvath
Cover Design by: Jessica Wei

Printed in China
Prime: U4077
ISBN: 979-8-88603-334-2

CONTENTS

Introduction 9
Restored 10
Never Too Late 12
Imperfect But Loved 14
God Is in It 16
Trust in the Restoration Process 18
Make God Your Focus 20
Forgiving Others 22
Let Me Be Perfect 24
Forgiving Self 26
Keep Your Eyes on Jesus 28
God's Timing 32
Saying No 34
Saying Sorry 36
Worthy of Friendship 38
Jumping to Conclusions 40
Surrender 42
Pruning 44
Staying Humble 46
Follow Him 48
Not Alone 50

Open the Door 54
Faith Roots 56
Starting Over 58
Pleasing Others 60
Your Needs 62
Letting Go of Expectations 64
Go Live 66
False Idols 68
Rhythm of Life 70
Accepting Your Life 72
Letting It Go 76
Restoration Through God 78
Feeling Guilty 80
You Are Worthy 82
Take Time for You 84
You Have a Purpose 86
Getting Stronger 88
Loving Yourself 90
The Heart 92
Finding Your Voice 94
Things Take Time 98
The Light 100
Grass Isn't Always Greener 102
Thoughts of Others 104

Be Joyful 106
Restoring Your Faith 108
Carrying the Weight 110
Others' Burdens 112
Praising Through It 114
Feeling Love 116
Loving Others 120
For the Lord 122
I Get to Do This 124
Not by Works 126
Repenting 128
Restoring Your Soul 130
Your Thoughts 132
Overcoming the World 134
Prayer 136
Rest in Restoration 138
Seeing God in It 142
Be Still 144
Fruit of the Spirit 146
Judging Others 148
Be Okay with Change 150
Restoring What Was Lost 152
Being Made New 154
Not Feeling Loved 156

Trust in Others 158
A Heart of Love 160
You Are Who 164
Jesus over Everything 166
Your Gifts 168
Releasing Your Past 170
Healing 172
Cleansing from Sin 174
Restoring Us to Him 176
Dancing in the Rain 178
Being Right 180
Feeling Bad About 182
Live Your Life 186
Own Way versus God's Way 188
Weeds 190
Cleanse the Heart 192
Accepting Peace 194
Stop the Cycle 196
Be Transformed 198
Living in the Flesh 200
Goodbye to Your Old Self 202
Embracing Your New 204

INTRODUCTION

It's easy to go about life each day and not realize that we, too, are broken. We're not perfect. We take a look inside ourselves and see there are areas we want to fix, areas where we want to be better—for ourselves, as well as for our families and friends. God can help us fix those areas and become better, renewing the light in us even when we can only see darkness. Events or things that have come our way do not have to define us. Today, you can know that you don't have to walk this path alone.

God is our Healer and our Redeemer, and He has the ability to fix and transform us. Friend, I'm honored to walk beside you as you become restored and embrace your new. So grab a fresh, hot cup of coffee or tea, and let's do this!

Cheers!
Melissa

@melissa_horvath_

@sweetwaterdecor

Nº. 01

RESTORED

After you have suffered a little while, the God of all grace, who has called you to his eternal glory in Christ, will himself restore, confirm, strengthen, and establish you.

I PETER 5:10

This is a little story of how this devotional came to be. When I was at a church retreat and singing worship music, God gave me a beautiful vision. He kept telling me to go up and share this vision with the others there. I sat there nervously for a while, then decided to obey His calling. So I raised my hand to share, stood up, and walked to the front of the room. I asked the women in the audience to close their eyes and imagine this scene with me.

"Picture yourself as a wooden dresser being made by the Lord—so beautiful, created of new wood, maybe with some artistic carvings," I said. "But over the years, you end up getting some dings, you're painted over a few times, and because of life's wear and tear, you end up looking like something that's been put along the side of the road for free.

"Now picture this: Jesus is carrying you to His workshop. As you see the light coming in from the dusty windows, He gently strips off all that paint, fills in the dings, and restores you to reveal what was hidden underneath all along . . . so you can see yourself how you are seen by the Lord, restored to your former glory."

Friend, we all are broken, and we can all be restored, just as that dresser was, in Christ. The holes will never be perfect, but they can be filled. We all go through a lot in life, but we can be made new by our Creator. We can make a choice to continue down a road that doesn't serve us, or we can take a new path of healing and restoration.

Embrace Your New

Today is the day when you enter the workshop. Take a look around, get used to the surroundings, and know that God is with you, always. In time, He will begin to strip off all the paint, allowing you to get real with yourself and embrace a new you—one that has been hidden inside. The journey isn't an easy one, but let me tell you, friend, it will be worth it.

Nº. 02

NEVER TOO LATE

This is the day that the Lord has made;
let us rejoice and be glad in it.
PSALM 118:24

You may be reading this devotion thinking, *I'm too old or too set in my ways to start something new now.* Or you may be thinking that too much time in your life has passed, and now it's too late to make any changes or start anything new. Friend, take refuge in Psalm 118 . . . today is a new day! It's never too late to begin again. It's never too late to receive healing, restoration, and the gift of being made new by your Lord and Savior! He's there, waiting with open arms for you to come on in. You can do the things He's placed on your heart . . . He will make the next steps clear for you and direct you to take them.

No matter how much time has passed, we can make the active choice right now to make any changes in our lives that we need to make. Each day brings about new opportunities, and it's up to us to make those moves! Philippians 4:13 reminds us: "I can do all things through him who strengthens me." He is with you, and He can give you strength. Push away any doubt the enemy is trying to feed you, and go forward as the new you, ready to say "yes!" to whatever new things God is leading you to do! It's never too late to change your life. You're never too old to enter the workshop and let the Lord begin to restore you.

Embrace Your New

Think of this process as if you'd come out of a hair salon with a new look. As you come out restored, others will notice and want to know "where you went" so they can "get the look too." This becomes your opportunity to spread the Word, letting others hear your story and learn about Jesus. You can use your story as a testimony to let others know that they aren't alone and that we are all broken. Don't let the enemy stand in your way of healing and being made new. It's never too late to move forward into the light!

N°. 03

IMPERFECT BUT LOVED

God knows that when you eat from it your eyes will be opened, and you will be like God, knowing good and evil.

GENESIS 3:5 NIV

Back in the book of Genesis, Adam and Eve lived in a beautiful garden where all of their needs were met, and they didn't know anything about evil. They were in perfect harmony with God and each other. There was no conflict, just one simple command from God: Do not eat of the tree of knowledge of good and evil. But the serpent slyly tricked Eve, and she ate the fruit of the tree, and after that Adam did too. They then knew of both good and evil. However, God still loved them, despite their disobedience.

As you take a look at your own story and that of your family, you can see that we are all products of imperfect people. We can often feel, too, past wounds that never healed but were maybe just sealed up or buried. As our own eyes open to knowing what's good and what's evil, God can help us stop generational pains as He shows us how they have affected us and how they may be starting to affect the next generation.

Remember, God can exchange pain for glory. While we can't go back to our own past (or the lives of those before us) and change things, we can decide how we choose to live today. God loves you, even in your questioning, even in your darkest moments. He wants you to draw nearer to Him.

Embrace Your New

As you look to God for restoration, pray for Him to reveal what needs light shed on it. Whether things from the past or recent occurrences, ask Him to show you what needs healing. There may be more than one thing or area, but take heart and know that none of us is perfect. Close your eyes and lay those places that need healing at God's feet. Decide with a full heart to give Him any and all of the pain that you hold, and with faith, believe that He's working in and through it. After all, who better to care for and heal your heart than your Creator?

N°. 04

GOD IS IN IT

For we are his workmanship, created in Christ Jesus for good works, which God prepared beforehand, that we should walk in them.

EPHESIANS 2:10

Unfortunately, life isn't always easy. The Old Testament is full of accounts of pain and suffering but God's will prevailing. One story I've been captivated by is the life of Joseph—his brothers wanted to kill him, but they ended up selling him into slavery instead. After a short period of time spent rising to prominence, he was falsely accused and thrown into prison. Even in captivity, Joseph's faithfulness gained him favor, and he was eventually appointed as the second-in-command to Pharaoh. He was put in charge of bringing Egypt out of a famine, and that's when his brothers showed up to ask for food:

> So Joseph said to his brothers, "Come near to me, please." And they came near. And he said, "I am your brother, Joseph, whom you sold into Egypt. And now do not be distressed or angry with yourselves because you sold me here, for God sent me before you to preserve life. For the famine has been in the

land these two years, and there are yet five years in which there will be neither plowing nor harvest. And God sent me before you to preserve for you a remnant on earth, and to keep alive for you many survivors. So it was not you who sent me here, but God. He has made me a father to Pharaoh, and lord of all his house and ruler over all the land of Egypt. (Genesis 45:4–8)

As we go through difficult times, we can remember how Joseph looked to God and believed that He is in it all—even when we don't yet have the answers—working through everything for His greater plan. The same is true for us: We may not know why we go through trials, but He does—and that's where our faith comes in.

Embrace Your New

Have you ever wondered, Why me? *When Joseph was sold into slavery by his brothers, he felt the pain, but he decided to live out each day for God. We might not be able to control our situations, but we* can *choose how we will react to them. God can turn times of trial into blessings and use them for His glory, even years later. Just as He saw Joseph through, He will see you through too.*

N°. 05

TRUST IN THE RESTORATION PROCESS

Agree with God, and be at peace; thereby good will come to you. Receive instruction from his mouth, and lay up his words in your heart.

JOB 22:21-22

Picture a box. Inside contains everything you carry . . . everything you don't want to give up control over—all your fears, worries, and anxieties. All things from your past that continue to be unresolved, people you have not forgiven, things God called you to do but you decided not to do—you knew better and went your own way instead. Friend, the key to open and set free everything held captive in that box is to give it over to God and fully have faith that He will lead your life. You can trust Him in what He's doing.

How? you might ask. The first step to trusting God is to know who He is. If you know God's character—if you know He is loving, faithful, and unchanging (Psalm 100:5; Hebrews 13:8)—then it's easier to trust Him with what's in your box.

You can say "yes!" to the callings and directions He has for you rather than thinking you can figure it out yourself. You can come to terms with how your life has played out, whether by your own choices or other people's doings, and take the path that follows Him rather than choosing to go your own way. You can make the choice today to trust in His restoration process and follow His ways.

Embrace Your New

Do you trust God—like, really *trust God—even with everything that came to mind as you pictured your box? Trust is so important in this restoration process. If you find that you lack trust in God, it's okay. You're not alone in this. You can build your trust by seeking to learn more about God's nature through the Bible, prayer, and personal experiences. Read about His promises. (Isaiah 41:10; Philippians 4:19; and Romans 8:28 are good places to start.) Pray and surrender. Only then can you fully trust His restoration process and find peace.*

N°. 06

MAKE GOD YOUR FOCUS

"Everyone then who hears these words of mine and does them will be like a wise man who built his house on the rock. And the rain fell, and the floods came, and the winds blew and beat on that house, but it did not fall, because it had been founded on the rock."

MATTHEW 7:24–25

Where do you turn for peace when you've had a hard day? In today's world, it's easy to find refuge in other people—friends or family members—or even worrying more about what other people think of us than what God does. Worrying about others' opinions of us is one sure way to lose our peace fast, but if we want to give our hearts peace and rejuvenation, we can always turn to God on our hard days, knowing that He is the Rock on which we can build the foundation of our emotions, our feelings—but especially our faith.

Bringing your soul to God and putting Him and His thoughts toward you first in your life can truly help you find the peace you need. And fostering your relationship with

Him—building a strong foundation by reading His Word, maintaining a healthy prayer life, attending a faith-filled body of believers regularly, and listening to and obeying His voice—is the best way to live the life of purpose and joy that He has for you. Do you put Him first in your life? Does His opinion matter more to you than the opinions of family or friends? Renew your trust in Him today—His plans are best, and His purposes for you are for good!

Embrace Your New

When was the last time you stopped to pray and just thank God for something He's done for you? Not ask Him for anything—but just share with Him something wonderful that happened in your day? When you focus on your relationship with Him and put it first, you will want to share with Him both the good and the bad parts of your day—not just the problems with which you need help. Above all, remember that God is always there for you—you can trust Him! He loves you so very much!

Nº. 07

FORGIVING OTHERS

Be kind to one another, tenderhearted, forgiving one another, as God in Christ forgave you.

EPHESIANS 4:32

Is there someone you need to forgive today? Maybe the person who pulled out in front of you in traffic this morning, or someone who hurt you in a greater way, perhaps through a broken relationship, one that has caused years of pain. One way to try to forgive someone is to remind yourself that you don't know the full story behind everyone's actions. For instance, the person who pulled out in front of you might have not seen you until the last minute. (I think we've all been guilty of doing this!)

Let's look at an example in the New Testament where Peter asked Jesus how he should forgive.

> Then Peter came up and said to him, "Lord, how often will my brother sin against me, and I forgive him? As many as seven times?" Jesus said to him, "I do not say to you seven times, but seventy-seven times." (Matthew 18:21–22)

We are all imperfect beings, living in a fallen world. Forgiveness is not forgetting, but intentionally releasing the person from any negative feelings you have toward them. And at the same time, when you forgive someone, it releases you from the same.

We all deserve forgiveness. Often we can think things that happen to us were caused because people intentionally meant to hurt us, but that isn't always the case. When we choose to control how we react, we are able to decide, with a true heart, to forgive others—just as Jesus forgives us.

Embrace Your New

Forgiveness is hard, but it's necessary for healing. You can start small. Think of a situation that you are still holding on to, and make the heart-and-soul decision to forgive that person. In a few days, notice how forgiveness has lessened the hold it's had on your soul and how it has affected your happiness and well-being. Then dig deeper into the bigger stuff and let it go. *I love closing my eyes and picturing myself giving my resentment and hurt feelings to Jesus, telling Him that I can't carry it any longer as I forgive those who have hurt me. I hope, friend, that today you can start forgiving, just as Jesus has forgiven you.*

Nº. 08

LET ME BE PERFECT

For by grace you have been saved through faith. And this is not your own doing; it is the gift of God, not a result of works, so that no one may boast.

EPHESIANS 2:8-9

Do you find yourself striving for perfection? Whether it was getting straight A's back in school, or today having a spotless house. It's easy to get stuck in a "perfection zone," trying to make sure every single task is flawlessly executed. But God says: "Let Me be perfect." *Wow*, isn't that a relief? We don't have to be perfect, because God is. All we need to do is rest in the fact that the God who deeply loves and cares for every detail of our lives *is* perfect.

Knowing that God is perfect in all His ways is important to the restoration process. Because we are human, we aren't meant to be perfect. In fact, the only perfect human to ever walk this earth was Jesus—not you, and not me. Doesn't that take the weight off?

You will have areas in which you fall short—and that's okay! God doesn't judge you if the house isn't cleaned up perfectly, or if you didn't get all the tasks checked off your to-do list—so why would you be so upset about it? Remember—God's love is not earned, and you cannot simply do works to enter the kingdom of heaven. He loves everything about you, including the mess inside your soul—and out! So the next time your finances don't work out perfectly, or the dinner you planned didn't come together, instead of being hard on yourself, remember: God is perfect, and He's got this. You can rely on Him.

Embrace Your New

What is the cause of your striving? Do you do it for the approval of others, or for God to see how hard you're working, or do you just enjoy the sense of accomplishment when it all comes together as planned? Whatever it may be, the next time you find yourself in the "perfection zone," all frazzled and stressed out, breathe. Take a step back and know that you are worthy, loved, and accepted by God–imperfections and all. And that is truly all that matters.

N°. 09

FORGIVING SELF

If we confess our sins,
he is faithful and just to forgive us our sins and
to cleanse us from all unrighteousness.

1 JOHN 1:9

Do you look back on a particular moment or season of your life and wish you could just erase it? Do you try to put it out of your mind, stuff it down like it didn't happen? The pressure that comes with shame and guilt is real. It can weigh us down and stop us from moving forward. Is it time to forgive yourself? Is it time to let go of feelings of less-than and open the door to healing and restoration? Right now, let it all out to the Lord—the good, the bad, the ugly, whatever you are carrying with you. Tell God that you are fully sorry—then ask for His grace, direction, and forgiveness. You can be real with Him, because He already knows your heart. Confess your sins, taking responsibility for them. If you've done this, then God has forgiven you. You are as pure as snow in His sight. And now for the hard part: It's time to forgive yourself. Be honest with yourself. It happened. It wasn't your finest hour.

Maybe you were doing the best you could at the time? Maybe you are not the same person you used to be? Make amends with others, if you need to. Understand that no one is perfect, and making mistakes doesn't make you a bad person. It may take time to fully release your feelings of guilt and regret. Be patient with yourself, silence your inner critic, and open your heart to this process of growth and healing. God is not holding anything over your head. Remember my analogy of the dresser? Picture one of your "dings" or holes being filled in and restored today—it may still be there, but as you let the grace of God cover you and begin to forgive yourself, you'll watch that hole be repaired. It's time to move forward, my friend, and that means leaving some old things behind.

Embrace Your New

Friend, I hope the act of surrendering it all to Him, asking for forgiveness, and forgiving yourself, helped lift some of the weight off you. Remember, you can do this at any time! Just as we learned in the previous devotion about forgiving others, Jesus said to forgive others seventy-seven times, and that's at least how much God will forgive you too. He loves you. Accept the gift of everlasting love from your heavenly Father, and take an amazing step today toward becoming new.

Nº. 10

KEEP YOUR EYES ON JESUS

Do not be anxious about anything, but in everything by prayer and supplication with thanksgiving let your requests be made known to God. And the peace of God, which surpasses all understanding, will guard your hearts and your minds in Christ Jesus.

PHILIPPIANS 4:6–7

We often keep our gaze on the situation at hand rather than keeping our focus on the Lord. I love this reminder of Peter going to Jesus by walking on the water:

> And Peter answered him, "Lord, if it is you, command me to come to you on the water." He said, "Come." So Peter got out of the boat and walked on the water and came to Jesus. But when he saw the wind, he was afraid, and beginning to sink he cried out, "Lord, save me." Jesus immediately reached out his hand and took hold of him, saying to him, "O you of little faith, why did you doubt?" And when they got into the boat, the wind ceased. And those

in the boat worshiped him, saying, "Truly you are the Son of God." (Matthew 14:28–33)

So, friend, why do you have little faith? Why do you keep your gaze on the wind that's swirling around you rather than on the One who settles the storm? You need to keep your eyes on Jesus and align your heart with His! It is something that does take practice, but when you decide to hand over even the smallest things to Him to handle instead of adding it to your own worry pile, it makes a difference. It helps build your faith in God as you release the situation at hand into His care. Like Peter attempting to walk on water, Jesus wants us to focus on Him, not at what's going on around us. He longs for us to live free of anxiety and worry, because He's working through it all. He wants us to be free of the stress and filled with His peace.

Embrace Your New

Friend, where do you need to refocus your gaze in life? What has been stealing your joy and causing you to be anxious? Today, choose to actively focus your gaze on the Lord and give over to Him anything that is stealing your joy or causing you to worry. Relax and live in the peace that only God can give. Remember, He's got this.

God gave us
a spirit
not of fear
but of
power and love
and self-control.

II Timothy 1:7

N°. 11

GOD'S TIMING

Wait for the L*ORD; be strong,*
and let your heart take courage;
wait for the L*ORD!*
PSALM 27:14

No one likes to wait for things. As kids, we have a hard time waiting for snack time, and as adults, we have a hard time waiting for the promotion we so obviously earned. In a world where we can order groceries online and have them delivered to our doorstep in a matter of hours, why would we *suffer* by waiting in line at the register?

While we continue to find ways to avoid the waiting experience, it's important to know that sometimes God wants us to sit tight and trust His timing. Also, we don't always get to know *why* He is asking us to wait or *why* we didn't get the answer we wanted after we waited for it.

I bet you can remember being told no by your parents, and looking back, you can see they were looking after you. They didn't give you something, because they knew it was better that you didn't have it. Friend, it is very humbling and reassuring to realize that God will keep you from things that are not meant for you—things that are not a part of His plan. Even though He gives you the freedom to make decisions for yourself, He is involved in your life. He already knows what's in your heart—and what's in everyone else's too.

Release the need for control over the timing of your life, the need to control what happens next in your life. Try to have patience in this waiting season, but also know that "for everything there is a season, and a time for every matter under heaven" (Ecclesiastes 3:1).

Embrace Your New

God's timing is not our timing. The Bible says, "With the Lord one day is as a thousand years, and a thousand years as one day" (II Peter 3:8). God knows you and *your heart, and He's working in and through all things, from the beginning of time to the end of time. Releasing control and allowing Him to work in His perfect timing is an important part of aligning your heart with His and becoming restored.*

N°. 12

SAYING NO

"Let what you say be simply 'Yes' or 'No'; anything more than this comes from evil."
MATTHEW 5:37

Do you ever have a hard time saying no? Maybe it's taking on something extra at work or at home, when your heart is really saying, "I just can't." Because even when we're worn out, we don't want to hurt others' feelings or let them down. Sometimes we say yes out of fear of what others will think of us—after all, we don't want to be seen as selfish or lazy. So, we choose to take on more even when we probably shouldn't.

Think about it this way: Do you think Jesus did things because of what others would think? If so, He wouldn't have gone near the tax collectors or the sinners. Friend, He went to them anyway, not worried about what others would think. And because Jesus knew with His whole heart that His mission was to fulfill the will of His Father.

It all goes back to the heart. There is a difference between doing something wholeheartedly and doing something you feel compelled to do. We can say yes to helping others when we are fully invested in it, doing it with a genuine passion that is fueled by God. Sometimes when God encourages you to say *yes*, you will feel an inner peace and confidence with your answer instead of an underlying dread. Ask yourself, *Does this project or task align with my God-given gifts?* If you have no passion for it, if you feel fear or dread, and/or if the task is not something in your wheelhouse, then it's okay to say no.

As we become restored by God, we can start being true to ourselves. We don't have to live our lives focused on pleasing others. Just because we *can* do something doesn't mean we *should*. We can sometimes say no, leaning into God to help us make our choices.

Embrace Your New

Today you can start living free from the fear of what others think of you. Say no to things that you're too tired to do or don't have it in your heart to do. It isn't your job to take care of all the emotions of everyone around you.

Nº. 13

SAYING SORRY

"Truly, truly, I say to you,
a servant is not greater than his master,
nor is a messenger greater than the one who sent him."
JOHN 13:16

As I was leaving a restaurant recently, someone held open the door for me and my kids to walk through, and I said, "Sorry!" And then I immediately questioned my response. *Why did I apologize for that?* After that, I started noticing the word "sorry" being used everywhere I went. It made me start wondering if being sorry for walking through a door that was opened for me was an issue of worth. When we say "sorry," is it because we don't feel worthy of kindness? Or because we feel less-than those around us? If that is the case, then we need to look to the Bible for what is true. God says we are worthy, beautiful, and important. And John 13:16 says that no one on earth is better than anyone else.

Rather than having an *I'm sorry* attitude, we should take a posture of gratitude. Next time you feel the urge to say, "I'm sorry," say, "Thank you!" And if you find yourself constantly apologizing and saying sorry because you feel less worthy or compelled to do so, go back to the heart. Remember, you were made in the image of God, and so was the other person.

On the other hand, if you truly wronged someone, it may be time to apologize. Do you need to check your heart for ways you have hurt others today? Do you need to find forgiveness and peace? If you are genuinely sorry for your actions, go to the other person, take responsibility, apologize, and ask for forgiveness. While this interaction may be uncomfortable, it is so necessary. Romans 14:19 gives us a great reminder: "So then let us pursue what makes for peace and for mutual upbuilding."

Embrace Your New

We are all in different situations and stages in life. Do you find yourself bringing down your own self-worth and apologizing to everyone for anything remotely involving you? If so, remember that John 13:16 says none of us is better than the other, and none of us is perfect. Do you truly need to approach someone with a full-hearted apology? Keep Romans 14:19 in mind. Pursue peace and mutual upbuilding to experience freedom today!

Nº. 14

WORTHY OF FRIENDSHIP

"Look at the birds of the air:
they neither sow nor reap nor gather into barns,
and yet your heavenly Father feeds them.
Are you not of more value than they?"

MATTHEW 6:26

You were created in the image of God, beautifully and wonderfully made. It's okay to have a different opinion or a unique skill. It's okay to enjoy what others might consider a chore. It's okay to be good at some things and not so good at others. You are you, not anyone else.

As we make our way through this life, it's easy to compare ourselves to others. We may feel unworthy of a certain person's friendship or not be our true selves to try to fit in with a group. But the truth is, we are worthy, with or without anyone's approval. We are worthy of love, friendship, and peace. Do you not believe it? Ask God to reveal the special ways He is working in your life, the unique gifts He has placed inside you, and to help you see your true worth. It may be that when you find yourself standing in who God made you to be, people will be attracted to your light—people whom you can be your true self with, people who will accept you, just as you accept them. We are meant to live in connection with others. But if the people you are hanging around don't see how truly amazing you are, then it may be time to take a step back from the group and reevaluate.

Embrace Your New

We can so often believe negative things we feel about ourselves or think others feel about us instead of the good things that God believes about us. Let's change that mindset–the next time you hear your inner critic, call it out for what it is. And then speak truth to it: I am worthy of love. I am worthy of good relationships. I am worthy of happiness. I am worthy of peace. *Allow the Lord to help you strip away all the falsehoods and replace them with the truth of His love for you.*

No. 15

JUMPING TO CONCLUSIONS

Be not quick in your spirit to become angry, for anger lodges in the heart of fools.
ECCLESIASTES 7:9

Do you ever find yourself jumping to conclusions? For instance, maybe your friend didn't respond to your message right away, so she must be mad at you. Or you get one piece of negative feedback at work, and in your mind, it negates all the positive feedback you've received over the years, leaving you thinking, *I must be terrible at my job.*

I do it too! Recently, I saw white spots on the new rug in the bathroom. *Bleach*, I thought. *I trusted someone to clean the bathroom and they ruined the rug . . . in multiple spots.* But later, when I used a wet cloth, the white spots wiped off. I'd jumped to conclusions and built up an entirely untruthful scenario about the situation that took away the joy in my soul, but it turns out, I was able to fix it quickly.

Let's face it—we've all jumped to conclusions without thinking things through. But what if instead we started viewing the world with a lens of grace? What if we started approaching life, people, and situations with a mindset characterized by compassion, forgiveness, and understanding rather than judgment, criticism, or harshness? It involves resisting the urge to jump to conclusions, and instead choosing to approach situations with curiosity and an open heart. Living with this mindset would foster deeper connections, reduce conflict, and create a more supportive, compassionate environment. It might even heal wounds and bridge divides. Think it's worth a try?

Embrace Your New

In order to be renewed, we need to learn from Ecclesiastes about not being quick to become angry. We receive another great reminder of this in Proverbs 19:11: "Good sense makes one slow to anger, and it is his glory to overlook an offense." God calls us many times in the Bible to be slow to anger and not to let the sun go down on our anger. God knows we can easily become upset, for He created us and our hearts. He knows that when we're feeling frustrated, it is best for us to slow down and not jump to conclusions and let anger overtake us. Instead, we can be filled by Him with grace and a spirit of forgiveness.

Nº. 16

SURRENDER

Trust in the Lord with all your heart,
and do not lean on your own understanding.
In all your ways acknowledge him,
and he will make straight your paths.
PROVERBS 3:5–6

A part of becoming renewed is making the decision to surrender your own plans and embrace God's plan. Maybe you thought you'd be married by now or have a certain career . . . but friend, He is working in and through it all. He knows *your* heart. Sometimes we think that if what we want hasn't happened yet, then it's a "no," but that isn't always the case. God could still be preparing that job, relationship, or whatever it is for you. We will never fully understand His timing, but we can still decide to surrender control of it all to Him.

As you're reading this, take a deep breath in and exhale out all that control you're carrying in your mind, heart, body, and soul—all those feelings about wanting things to go your own way, in your own timing. You may wonder why you're in the season you're experiencing, but friend, there is a *purpose* for it all. You may need to go through this trial to grow deeper in your faith and reliance on Him, or you may need to learn something from your current job so you'll be prepared for the next one, which will happen in God's perfect timing. You may simply be needing to learn patience and surrender. No matter what, know that you can always trust God with your life.

Embrace Your New

Today marks a perfect turning point and opportunity in your faith walk. I hope and pray you have thought of areas in your life where you have been holding tight to control and have now decided it's time to surrender. When the timing is right, God will move in your life, and it's up to you to say "yes!" to that next step. Remember, friend, He's working in everyone's life—not just yours. He has created a beautiful, orchestrated symphony in which we each are playing our own instruments. Often, we can only hear our own music playing, but if we could watch the symphony from above, we'd be able to hear the beautiful sound of God directing everyone together.

N°. 17

PRUNING

"I am the true vine, and my Father is the vinedresser. Every branch in me that does not bear fruit he takes away, and every branch that does bear fruit he prunes, that it may bear more fruit. Already you are clean because of the word that I have spoken to you. Abide in me, and I in you. As the branch cannot bear fruit by itself, unless it abides in the vine, neither can you, unless you abide in me. I am the vine; you are the branches. Whoever abides in me and I in him, he it is that bears much fruit, for apart from me you can do nothing."

JOHN 15:1–5

Did you know that when you prune off certain branches of tomato plants, it helps the nutrients flow to the fruit rather than to the unfruitful branches? With dahlias, if you prune them when they get to a certain height, they will produce more flowers. The same goes for you, friend. God prunes people, jobs, situations, relationships, and more out of your life so you can grow. You may not understand your current circumstance, but the process will always help you grow closer to Him rather than farther away.

You can also do some pruning—so take a look at your life and see what needs to be pruned. Are you giving too much of your time and energy to something that is no longer serving you? Are you doing something that you wish you'd said no to, but you didn't want to upset someone else? When you experience pruning in your life, come back to the verses in John 15:1–5 and read them over a few times, remembering that God is working through it all.

Embrace Your New

As you do some pruning in your own life, understand that you don't have to do it all, carry it all, or overextend yourself. As God does His pruning, choose to praise Him rather than question Him. Imagine God telling you, "If only you knew what I have for you next!" Then get out your Bible and read Ecclesiastes 3:1–8. Remember, there is a reason and a season for everything and every purpose—including times of pruning.

N°. 18

STAYING HUMBLE

Humble yourselves,
therefore, under the mighty hand of God
so that at the proper time he may exalt you,
casting all your anxieties on him,
because he cares for you.
I PETER 5:6–7

Let's take a closer look at the first part of this passage: *being humble and humbling yourself before God*. Friend, although it sometimes doesn't feel like it, God is working all things out for your good and for His plan. Look back at your life and think about all the times when God showed up in ways that only *He* could have. Giving Him thanks and glory during the pruning process can feel counterintuitive, but lifting His name high during this new season is only going to draw you closer to your comforting Creator.

Whether your "new" is a hard change or an exciting one, don't forget to give credit where credit is due: God has brought you this far, working through you. This doesn't mean you shouldn't assess how far you've come or celebrate accomplishments. It only means that you get to celebrate all that you did by aligning with the God of the universe. You are celebrating the bigger picture.

Now let's take a look at the second part of this passage: *casting all your anxieties on Him, because He cares for you.* Friend, you don't have to worry about what is next for you. You don't have to put one second of thought into what could go wrong. Talk to God, asking Him to carry the weight for you. He doesn't want you to live in fear—He cares deeply for you; He will never leave you; and He has great plans for this season of your life—and the next one as well.

Embrace Your New

*In this season of transition, stay grounded by continually acknowledging that it is God who is guiding you and providing for you. Other ways to stay humble include serving others (even in small ways) and staying open to learning. Remember that everything you have, including this new season, is a gift from Him. By staying humble, you can face this transition with peace, knowing that He is with you every step of the way. Trust the process–*His *process–and you will look back someday to see the pieces coming together in your life in a wonderful way.*

Nº. 19

FOLLOW HIM

And he said to all, "If anyone would come after me,
let him deny himself and
take up his cross daily and follow me."
LUKE 9:23

Luke 9:23 outlines the steps we need to take in order to embrace change. It reminds us to deny ourselves, meaning to surrender our plans and desires to God's will and trust His path for us. And if we truly want to fully embrace this newness, we may need to let go of some old comforts, habits, and expectations. Sometimes the loss of what is familiar—whether it's a job, a relationship, or a lifestyle—can lead to a deeper experience of life and our purpose in Christ.

The Scripture also tells us that the person who follows Jesus must "take up his cross daily." The cross represents sacrifice, suffering, and a willingness to endure hardship. So to "take up his cross daily" means to remain faithful and steadfast, accepting that change may involve sacrifice and growth. Being reshaped or remade can be uncomfortable at best and downright painful at worst. But it's important to remember that while we can accept pain as part of the process, we can also lean into God's strength rather than relying on our own.

After we deny ourselves and take up our cross, we are told to "follow him"—to trust Him, to stay close to Him, to read His Word, to pray, to listen, and to follow through when He nudges us in one direction or another (even if it is in a direction we never thought we'd go). We can trust that He is leading us toward something better.

Embrace Your New

Going back to our very first devotion, as you enter the workshop, you have to be okay *with the Lord renewing you. You have to take a breath in and out, which may be hard, as He strips away the old paint and starts to fill in the cracks. But, friend, it will be worth it. Today, accept His invitation into a fresh, new relationship with God.*

N°. 20

NOT ALONE

Let us consider how to stir up one another to love and good works, not neglecting to meet together, as is the habit of some, but encouraging one another, and all the more as you see the Day drawing near.

HEBREWS 10:24-25

We can often think we're the only ones who feel the way we do . . . and we can often be the hardest on ourselves. But, friend, you are not alone. You are not the only one who picked up this book feeling the need to be restored and to become new in Christ. Remember, He's walking with you always and is always there for you.

Finding community and friends with whom you can share your real self is important. God wants us to have others in our lives. Having friends and community is not just for our own sake but for their sake too. The Bible tells us to love, meet with, and encourage one another. I hope that as I write this to you, it feels to you like we're sitting and talking together, that I'm here listening to you and offering some advice in Christ. I encourage you to meet with others, to encourage them, and to share what you've learned to help lift them up.

Friend, never feel as if your brokenness is too heavy to

share with others. We are all broken. None of us is perfect, but by the grace of God, He forgives us and loves us, despite our thoughts and actions. True community and friendship go beyond the superficial as people connect with each other on a deeper level. You are deserving of that kind of community, friend. Know that you are worth so much and that you are not alone.

Embrace Your New

Today, I encourage you to think of your circle of friends. What does it look like? Do you feel like you truly have community? Take inventory and see where you can find deeper connections—whether that's with the friends you already have or by joining a new small group. Some of the greatest connections come from being around other believers who are also broken but are seeking community in order to be their real selves.

If I were still tryi

I would not be

please people,

rvant of Christ.

Galatians 1:10 NIV

No. 21

OPEN THE DOOR

Two are better than one, because they have a good reward for their toil. For if they fall, one will lift up his fellow. But woe to him who is alone when he falls and has not another to lift him up! Again, if two lie together, they keep warm, but how can one keep warm alone? And though a man might prevail against one who is alone, two will withstand him—a threefold cord is not quickly broken.

ECCLESIASTES 4:9–12

When hard change happens unexpectedly, it's common to want to isolate yourself—you stop answering the phone when your friends call; you stop showing up to Sunday dinners with family; you go to your room, pull the covers over your head, and distance yourself from the rest of the world. But Ecclesiastes 4:9–12 tells us there is *power* in community, mutual support, and unity. Renewal in Christ is often a process that requires reliance on others. Is it time to find the courage to let others into your process? What type of encouragement do you need? Do you need someone to just sit with you? Do you need someone who can give you an encouraging word? Do you need to be reminded of your faith? Or reminded of who you are? Make a list of the types of encouragement you need, then make a list of people who could give you the support you need to work through the situation

Sometimes the care of others—whether through prayer or simply being present—can be a means of experiencing God's love in a tangible way. Remember, He can bring just the right person at just the right time to give you a message straight from His heart. So maybe it's time to crawl out from under the covers, open the door, and let others know what you are going through. Then just see what happens.

Embrace Your New

Friend, you are not meant to journey alone. Open your heart to the support God provides through community. And don't forget to stay tuned in to those around you. Does someone in your circle suddenly seem closed off? You might just want to give them a call, letting them know they can lean on you when they are ready. God works through His people in the most amazing ways–you never know when you'll have the privilege to share God's love and care with someone who needs a reminder.

N°. 22

FAITH ROOTS

For you know that the testing of your faith produces steadfastness.

JAMES 1:3

I have some really old oak trees at my house. I look at them, thinking, *Wow, you have withstood so many storms, seen so many things, in the hundreds of years you've been here!* This got me to thinking about how strong and deep their roots must be to withstand all the storms in which other trees have fallen.

Friend, I love how God gives visual representations in creation of how we should live. As God continues to restore, renew, and re-create us, we know that through this process we are deepening and strengthening our faith roots. While it may not feel as if we are rooted right now, James 1:3 says the testing of our faith produces steadfastness. One day, others will be looking at us like I look at my old oak trees, wondering how we were able to withstand the storms that struck in our lives. And who knows? They may even be wowed enough to ask you about your journey, and you'll be given the opportunity to share your story and help spread the Gospel.

No one is exempt from trials and tribulations. And it's usually in the hard moments that we are faced with the decision to either grow closer to God or push Him away. It's so easy to get stuck in the pain of the past, the grief of losing someone you love, the dreams that never came true. You throw up your hands, wondering why God didn't come through in the way you wanted Him to. But, friend, when you actively decide to turn toward Him in these moments, you can grow closer to Him than ever before. He will lend you His strength to keep going. And ultimately, your faith roots will grow strong and deep, able to stand up to even the strongest winds.

Embrace Your New

You may be wondering how to deepen your faith roots outside of trials. Getting in God's Word can help you grow deeper. Participating in a "read the Bible in a year" program, listening to worship music, joining a Bible study group, reading a devotional (like you are right now!), or just simply talking with God can help grow you in your faith. Remember, a faith community is amazing to get plugged into, and most churches have small groups to join. You can even start one yourself! You can find many opportunities to deepen your faith when you look for them.

N°. 23

STARTING OVER

"Remember not the former things,
nor consider the things of old.
Behold, I am doing a new thing;
now it springs forth, do you not perceive it?
I will make a way in the wilderness
and rivers in the desert."
ISAIAH 43:18–19

Friend, I hope this journey to *embracing your new* is going well. I know there are always bumps in the road during any transition, but I wanted to say "great job" for making it this far! And congratulations!

Second Corinthians 5:17 says, "Therefore, if anyone is in Christ, he is a new creation. The old has passed away; behold, the new has come." Have you ever thought of yourself as a "new creation," free from your past pains, problems, stains, and failures? Now seen and felt as a bright, new, shiny beloved child of God, forgiven, redeemed, and set apart? It's hard to believe, I know, but it's true! Your slate is wiped clean. Take a moment to let this sink in. Believe it.

If you've fallen back into your old ways, don't worry. You can start over any day. God hasn't gone anywhere. He is still with you, holding out His arms, welcoming you to experience His restorative power. So lean in, accept this gift, and experience what true renewal means. I can assure you, it's a beautiful thing.

Embrace Your New

I hope you are already starting to feel made new and restored in your journey. When I think of starting over, this verse comes to mind: "Behold, I am doing a new thing; now it springs forth, do you not perceive it? I will make a way in the wilderness and rivers in the desert" (Isaiah 43:19). I encourage you to read through all the devotions in this book, and after you're done, look back on them as you need to throughout life. Remember, you can choose to start something new in you, each day. You can take each devotion and begin to apply it right after you read it. I'm excited that you're well on your way to embracing your new!

Nº. 24

PLEASING OTHERS

For am I now seeking the approval of man, or of God? Or am I trying to please man? If I were still trying to please man, I would not be a servant of Christ.

GALATIANS 1:10

As a people pleaser, I'm inclined to put myself last to make others happy. But if I'm being honest, doing this usually leaves me feeling worn out and unheard. As I have been on my own restoration journey, I have come to learn that I do not need to bend over backward at the expense of my own health. While *people-pleasing* is in my nature, the weight it leaves on my soul can be too heavy, so this is part of my own restoration process.

How about you? Do you agree with others even when you don't actually agree, just to avoid conflict? Do you go along with what everyone else wants so you won't be the odd one out? Do you often feel unappreciated or taken advantage of? Do you obsess over whether you might have offended someone after a conversation? If so, you might be a people pleaser as well.

It's important to remember that sometimes you need to take care of yourself first. One way to break the people-pleasing habit is to slowly start expressing your opinions, desires, and needs. If you have a different opinion, share it. If you want to go to a different restaurant than the group does, say it out loud with confidence. See what happens. You can learn that being assertive, and speaking what you think or feel in honesty, doesn't mean you're being aggressive. I think you'll find that those around you likely want to hear more from you. Lean into God for the strength to use your voice. It may be hard at first, but God can help you catch yourself when you're seeking to please others too much, and He can guide you in your actions (even if it seems counterintuitive).

Embrace Your New

This has probably been one of the toughest changes for me to make, and maybe it is for you too. It takes active awareness. The next time you start to cancel your own plans to help someone else, ask yourself if what you are doing is coming from a deep fear of rejection or a desire for acceptance. If it comes from either of those places, reconsider canceling your plans. It's time to put yourself back on the calendar.

N°. 25

YOUR NEEDS

Make every effort to live in peace
with everyone and to be holy;
without holiness no one will see the Lord.
See to it that no one falls short of the grace of God
and that no bitter root grows up
to cause trouble and defile many.

HEBREWS 12:14–15 NIV

At my company, Sweet Water Décor, I needed help, but instead of acknowledging this fact, I chose to do things myself. This put more on me than I could handle. Meanwhile, at home, I would feel bad if my husband didn't give me a hug or kiss. But instead of voicing these feelings, I would just let them fester. My hidden expectations turned into internalized frustration, and I was heading down a path to resentment. When I finally did share, it was such a relief.

The Bible encourages clear communication, mutual upbuilding, and honesty in relationships. It calls us to speak "the truth in love" (Ephesians 4:15), and to "make every effort to live in peace with everyone" (Hebrews 12:14), to see to it that no "bitter root grows up to cause trouble" (Hebrews 12:15). Friend, honesty is the key. Do you have hidden needs you haven't shared with anyone? Whether it be needing more help around the house, needing more affection from your spouse, or needing more personal space, don't wait for resentment to set in before letting your needs be known. Remember, you can let your needs be known and learn to be assertive in your life. Let the people in your life know what is going on in your head. Who knows? It may even open the door for your children, spouse, coworkers, and friends to let you know how you can best support them. And this, my friend, creates honest, lasting relationships that can last forever.

Embrace Your New

One of the most wonderful parts of restoration is no longer being held captive by your thoughts, feelings, or needs. You are an important child of God, and you owe it to yourself to be true to what you need. You can't expect other people to read your mind. Speak your needs and truth without putting a false belief on how another person will respond. Relief is waiting for you on the other side of that conversation.

Nº. 26

LETTING GO OF EXPECTATIONS

"They tie up heavy burdens, hard to bear,
and lay them on people's shoulders,
but they themselves are not willing
to move them with their finger."

MATTHEW 23:4

When I married my husband, I thought we'd have this beautiful, loving relationship—now and forever—the kind you often dream about when you're first deeply in love. A business and a few kids later, I thought, *Wait—I don't think he's living up to my expectations as my husband, or my lover, in his actions toward me.* We can state our needs, but we also need to temper our expectations. The reality is, people are the way they are at their core. They can change in some ways, but typically God made them to be how they are. I didn't marry someone who demonstrates love like you see in the movies, but I did marry the partner God had for me. We may not have the love you see in the movies, but as opposite as we are, God made our two puzzle pieces to fit together to be what each other needs in life—at home and at work!

For you, this may look different. Maybe you have expectations for situations or people in your life that you need to change. Realize that you can't always make them something they are not or were not ever meant to be. You may have had expectations for yourself to be promoted to the next level of your career by a certain time, or to be married and have kids by a certain age. It's time to surrender these earthly expectations to God. Let Him work in them, in His timing. Only when we surrender our human expectations will we experience peace and true freedom.

Embrace Your New

Friend, when I need a relaxing moment in life, I close my eyes and go to the beach in my mind. I see the beautiful sky and hear the wind and the waves crashing around me. Join me here . . . and as we look out to sea together, let's take our expectations and let the sea wash them all away. God will gather them up and sort through what's for us and what's not. It's a beautiful, soul-cleansing experience of letting go of anything we are holding on to and releasing any unrealistic expectations that we may have of life in this imperfect world. Remember, He's got this!

N°. 27

GO LIVE

Do not be anxious about anything,
but in everything by prayer and supplication
with thanksgiving let your requests
be made known to God. And the peace of God,
which surpasses all understanding, will guard
your hearts and your minds in Christ Jesus.

PHILIPPIANS 4:6–7

No matter what, we can hold on to this truth: God is good. He wants to walk with us in our suffering. We can trust Him, as He has a deep love for us. He has wonderful plans for us! As we go about life, we can be held down by things that plague us from our past or current situations we just can't seem to get through. Imagine looking ahead in your life, and ask yourself this: *Will things that are on my mind now still be affecting me then?*

Today, release to God anything that is stealing joy from your life. Then listen to what He is trying to tell you. He may be calling you to get deeper help through therapy or to receive more support by joining a small group. We can spend too much of our lives stuck in sadness, pain, anxiety, and worry, while God is inviting us to be released from these things.

There is hope and peace that can be found in God, and we can live happier, more fulfilling lives when we choose to follow Him. I love Jesus' words in John 14:27: "Peace I leave with you; my peace I give to you. Not as the world gives do I give to you. Let not your hearts be troubled, neither let them be afraid."

Embrace Your New

Friend, don't sit around and wait for better days. Choose today to allow restoration to take place. You can lessen your need to please others, and you can stop being held captive by anxiety and worry. Don't let fear hold you back from living the life God has given you. Trust me, I'm in it with you! When we actively choose to live in the light instead of in the darkness, we can receive the peace and happiness that God has for each of us.

N°. 28

FALSE IDOLS

Therefore, my beloved, flee from idolatry.

I CORINTHIANS 10:14

What comes to mind when you think of an "idol"? Is it a popular television singing contest? If so, you wouldn't be alone. Or you may recall the Israelites offering sacrifices to a golden calf after being delivered from Egypt. God wasn't very pleased about it. In Exodus 20:3–5, He told them: "You shall have no other gods before me. You shall not make for yourself a carved image, or any likeness of anything that is in heaven above, or that is in the earth beneath, or that is in the water under the earth. You shall not bow down to them or serve them, for I the LORD your God am a jealous God." You may be thinking, *Well, I don't do that!* Maybe so, but I bet you never thought your phone could be an idol. Or your perfect yard. Or your image.

Don't get me wrong. We are allowed to have passions, and we need to live out our purpose—just be wary of any false idols in your life. *Idolatry* is defined as the worship of someone or something other than God. The first of the Ten Commandments says: "You shall have no other gods before me." It goes on to say that those who commit idolatry include anyone who attaches to a creature the confidence, loyalty, and devotion that properly belong only to the Creator.

With this definition in mind, do you have any idols? The first step is to recognize and acknowledge that something or someone has become an idol in your life. Ask God for forgiveness, then ask Him to help you break *free*. By redirecting your focus and turning your eyes toward Jesus alone, you will be able to align your heart with His. And this, my friend, is a huge step in the restoration process.

Embrace Your New

Is there anything in your life that is—or may become—an idol, something you need to quit focusing on so you can redirect your attention to God? Today, pray to the Lord to reveal any false idols you may have in your life, and listen to the nudges He gives you.

Nº. 29

RHYTHM OF LIFE

For everything there is a season, and a time for every matter under heaven.

ECCLESIASTES 3:1

We all go through dormant seasons, when there is no growth and nothing seems to be happening, but God is still working behind the scenes. Though nothing may seem to be happening, God is actually preparing us for our next season of life. You need to remember, friend: God is working through it all—no matter what season you're in. Each of us needs the rain of the spring to bring out the flowers and the new growth in our lives.

Ironically, as I was writing this devotion, my daughter yelled to me, "Mom, why is the sun not out?" I said, "Well, it's meant to be cloudy right now." God has a purpose for *everything* under the sun—literally. Some days are meant to be cloudy, others rainy, others sunny . . . all for His greater plan—and for ours too. I love how, through nature, He can show us that seasons happen for a reason. We need both cloudy days and sunny days. But what a beautiful picture God paints through the different seasons and all kinds of weather. We may not understand why we're in a certain season when someone else is in another, but God does. We aren't meant to live someone else's life—we're meant to live our own life. He's working in you differently than He's working in someone else. But we are all here, together, experiencing the rhythm of life as we look to God.

Embrace Your New

Notice and accept the season you're in, and don't try to move ahead to that next season before you're ready. Soak up the clouds, rain, or sunshine that you are experiencing and know that God is preparing you for what's next. We don't have to know it all, but we can replace our feelings of worry with trust that God is carrying us through and that He is with us in each season of life. Ecclesiastes is such a wonderful reminder that there is a rhythm to life and a season for everything. A friend of mine is currently waiting to move into a new house—while the people in that *house are looking to find theirs. God is working it all out. There's a rhythm to life, and everything works together in* His *timing.*

Nº. 30

ACCEPTING YOUR LIFE

For all have sinned and fall short of the glory of God.
ROMANS 3:23

When I was playing golf with my husband the other day, I went up to the tee, set my ball on it, and took a hit with my driver. Let's just say it didn't go exactly where I wanted—it fell way short. I had a choice here: I could play the ball I had, or I could try again. God reminded me in that moment that this is a perfect representation of accepting the hand we've been dealt in life instead of ignoring it and trying to hit another ball. We may not be where we want to be in life, but it's where He's placed us, and we need to play the ball we've hit—no matter where it landed. This begins with accepting the circumstances of our lives—and accepting who we are. We cannot change the past, but we *can* change today.

As you go through the process of being restored and becoming made new, you can make the choice to accept your life and make decisions for yourself as you grow closer to God and learn more about Him. Romans 3:23 gives us a great reminder that we've all sinned and fallen short of the glory of God. Those in your family, your friends, and yes, you too, have sinned—and nobody is perfect. As you work through the restoration process, you will learn how to *live in* the now instead of in the past. If you find yourself stuck in past hurt and pain, I challenge you to seek further help to restore yourself—through therapy or a support group or another form of help. You can accept the circumstances of your life—both past and present—and with God's help, work toward a better future.

Embrace Your New

Take a deep breath in and out. Can you see and accept your life as it's played out so far? Can you make the choice today to continue on your restorative journey? Can you love yourself, just the way God made you? Friend, you are worthy–mess and all. I am with you–I am a mess too at times–and I pray you can find space to love yourself, love Jesus, and love others too, right where you're at.

The LORD is my shepherd;
I shall not want.
He makes me lie down
in green pastures.
He leads me beside
still waters.
He restores my soul.

Psalm 23:1-3

N°. 31

LETTING IT GO

Casting all your anxieties on him, because he cares for you.

I PETER 5:7

In this season of restoration, if anxiety and worry have weighed you down, please know that you're not alone. In fact, anxiety and worry have always been very real—even in Bible times. But I Peter 5:7 gives us hope that we can cast all our anxieties on the Lord as we let go of what is holding us back from a life of happiness.

Try writing down all that is stealing your joy—anxieties, worries, anything you need to give to God. Once you have your list written out, go through each item on it and pray to God, giving everything to Him. You can even have a bonfire, and when you're done praying, crumple up your list and throw it into the fire. Friend, as you *let go* of all that anxiety and worry, you will start to feel lighter, as you are actively walking in faith and trusting in God. Remember, there is no worry or anxiety that is too big for God. The next time you feel overcome with anxious thoughts, stop and bring them to Him.

Talk to Him—He wants to hear from you. He loves you, and He already knows your heart anyway, so there is nothing you need to hide. Let it go, and take that next beautiful step in your restoration process!

Embrace Your New

I hope that after today you can feel some of the weight lifted off your shoulders. God takes care of the birds and ensures they have food–and you are much more important to Him! (See Matthew 10:29–31.) You do not have to worry. Whenever you need a reminder of this, you can turn to Scriptures such as Proverbs 12:25: "Anxiety in a man's heart weighs him down, but a good word makes him glad." Here are a few more: John 14:27; Psalm 55:22; Philippians 4:6-7; Matthew 6:25-34; and Matthew 11:28-30.

N°. 32

RESTORATION THROUGH GOD

"The Lord is my shepherd; I shall not want. He makes me lie down in green pastures. He leads me beside still waters. He restores my soul. He leads me in paths of righteousness for his name's sake. Even though I walk through the valley of the shadow of death, I will fear no evil, for you are with me; your rod and your staff, they comfort me. You prepare a table before me in the presence of my enemies; you anoint my head with oil; my cup overflows."

PSALM 23:1-5

When you restore something, you help it to be renewed to its original condition. In fact, the word *restore* is mentioned many times in the Bible. John 10:10 gives us a beautiful reminder of this: "The thief comes only to steal and kill and destroy. I came that they may have life and have it abundantly." Those last words—"have life and have it abundantly"—can help us to know that no matter what we have been through, seeking the Lord can give us freedom and heal our minds and souls.

Hosea 6:1 says, "Come, let us return to the Lord; for he has torn us, that he may heal us; he has struck us down, and he will bind us up." The book of Psalms also teaches us about restoration. In one part of the Psalms, David was fleeing from King Saul, who was trying to hunt David down to kill him. Even in those trying times, David clung to the Lord and believed that He could restore his mind and soul. We can learn from David's story that we do not have to fear evil, because God is with us—always.

If you feel like God has forgotten about you in your trials, He has not. The Bible is filled with many stories of people who went through trials but who were still able to live a life *focused on God*. We can do the same thing! God wants us to come to Him and lean on Him, no matter the circumstances. He is the Restorer of our souls.

Embrace Your New

The book of Psalms is packed with so many inspiring words about loving God and learning to rely on Him to bring us through anything we're going through. Read through the psalms today and ask Him to heal any brokenness inside of you and to restore your soul.

Nº. 33

FEELING GUILTY

For by him all things were created,
in heaven and on earth, visible and invisible,
whether thrones or dominions or rulers or authorities—
all things were created through him and for him.

COLOSSIANS 1:16

Are you harboring any guilt in your heart? Maybe it's something from your past that plagues you daily. Have you ever experienced "mom guilt"? Or do you feel bad for not being able to make everyone happy all at once? Jesus died on the cross so that you wouldn't have to carry a heavy emotional burden. So that you could be set free from shame. God doesn't want you to hold on to the weight of guilt. He gave His Son to set you free from it.

You see, when you put your trust in Jesus, you are able to be transformed. Your identity is no longer defined by your past mistakes or your daily mishaps. You are made right with God, and that righteousness is not based on your works but on Jesus' perfect obedience. So, there's no need to live a guilt-centered life. Romans 8:1 (NIV) says, "Therefore, there is now no condemnation for those who are in Christ Jesus." So, ask for forgiveness, if need be, and release that weight you've been carrying around. Let it roll off your shoulders and fall to the ground. Because, as Romans 8:38–39 (THE MESSAGE) puts it, "Absolutely *nothing* can get between us and God's love because of the way that Jesus our Master has embraced us."

Embrace Your New

God can heal that hurt, friend. Romans 8:38–39 (THE MESSAGE) says, "Do you think anyone is going to be able to drive a wedge between us and Christ's love for us? There is no way! Not trouble, not hard times, not hatred, not hunger, not homelessness, not bullying threats, not backstabbing, not even the worst sins listed in Scripture." No matter what happened before this very minute, you are not too far gone. Picture Him restoring you, brokenness and all, with His love and grace and mercy. Today, ask God to forgive you for anything you are holding on to—any sin, any guilt, any shame—and to help you forgive yourself as well. As you are made new in Christ, you can let go of guilt and embrace the wonderful life He gives you.

N°. 34

YOU ARE WORTHY

For you formed my inward parts; you knitted me together in my mother's womb. I praise you, for I am fearfully and wonderfully made. Wonderful are your works; my soul knows it very well. My frame was not hidden from you, when I was being made in secret, intricately woven in the depths of the earth. Your eyes saw my unformed substance; in your book were written, every one of them, the days that were formed for me, when as yet there was none of them.

PSALM 139:13–16

We are not here by chance. We were thought up, by God, to be here, for so many wonderful purposes! Sometimes we can be the hardest on ourselves. Think of how you think of yourself, right now, and take note. Where have you put yourself down, one way or another? In what ways are you worried about what others think of you? Know that, when you do that, you are putting down something the Lord has made. This way of thinking is life-changing.

Isaiah 64:8 says, "But now, O Lord, you are our Father; we are the clay, and you are our potter; we are all the work of your hand." And Psalm 139:1–5 tells us: "O Lord, you have searched me and known me! You know when I sit down and when I rise up; you discern my thoughts from afar. You search out my path and my lying down and are acquainted with all my ways. Even before a word is on my tongue, behold, O Lord, you know it altogether. You hem me in, behind and before, and lay your hand upon me." God knows you and loves you, just the way you are! He knows your thoughts and your feelings—and He says *you are worthy*.

Friend, I hope you can love yourself and see yourself the way God sees you. Allow Him to change your heart-feelings, in your very soul, removing any negativity you might harbor toward yourself. He is the Potter, and you are the clay. He continues to mold you and shape you as you go through life.

Embrace Your New

Friend, you are worthy. Accept and receive the peace that comes from knowing that God has formed you and has so many wonderful purposes for you! You are beautifully and wonderfully made. Today, give God anything you're holding on to that is bringing you down rather than up. Ask Him to help you discover the life-changing love and peace you can receive from Him.

Nº. 35

TAKE TIME FOR YOU

Yet you do not know what tomorrow will bring. What is your life? For you are a mist that appears for a little time and then vanishes.

JAMES 4:14

Life is busy. We are constantly running here and there, trying to juggle school, work, kids, relationships, small groups, events, and so much more. With all this activity, it's easy to forget about ourselves. We try to do all we can to check off the boxes for others, and we're left wondering when *we* will be taken care of. It's important to carve out time for ourselves. A little quiet time before going to sleep or right when you wake up in the morning is a great way to relax. Reading Scripture, praying, and worshiping in silence reminds us of God's love in a very personal way. The time you set aside to connect with your Father is important. It gives you the energy and perspective you need for daily life.

Carving out time for yourself can also look like taking that class, going for that run, or eating that lunch out with a friend. After all, if you are giving all your energy to everyone else, you're off-balance. It's time to re-center your life so you can also take care of your own needs. You are worth it! It's okay to say no to that project or to get a sitter for the kids. It's okay to choose yourself, to be able to rest your soul a bit. Think of it like putting gas in a car. We simply cannot run on empty. We need to put fuel in our tanks so we can be refreshed and renewed to do all the things we have to do each day. We need to give ourselves permission to take a break from school or work or other responsibilities in order to let ourselves rest.

Embrace Your New

What do you love doing? When was the last time you did just that? We can always make a thousand excuses for not taking time for ourselves, but occasionally let's throw those excuses to the wind and instead advocate for ourselves to ourselves—you need time for you. *Even if it's something small, like taking a longer shower, going out to coffee by yourself, or treating yourself to ice cream (alone for once!) . . . take time for* you!

N°. 36

YOU HAVE A PURPOSE

The Lord will fulfill his purpose for me;
your steadfast love, O Lord, endures forever.
Do not forsake the work of your hands.

PSALM 138:8

When one season of life ends, you can feel scared, sad, excited, confused, and maybe even a bit lost, thinking, *Well, what's my purpose now?* You have so many wonderful purposes in this life. While you may not know exactly what is around the corner, it's important to look around at where you are right now. What does God have for you in this in-between stage of life? Should you volunteer more at church? What gifts has God given you that you could use in this season to bless others? While you may be waiting on a "big reveal" of what God is leading you to next, He may be calling you to look around and simply be where you're at.

You can also take this time to grow closer to Jesus, learning more and more about how He cares specifically for you. Over time, you will be able to notice when He nudges you—and when it's time to move forward, you'll be more confident in following His lead. You'll be able to recognize His voice over others who may want to influence your decisions. You'll be solid, standing on a strong foundation, and more aware of the bigger picture. You'll be fully prepared and ready to walk into the next big thing God has for you, without fear of failure. So take your time, serve others where you are, and deepen your relationship with your Father.

Embrace Your New

As you embrace the season of life you are in, be still and know that God has many purposes for you! And He will fulfill each of them. Don't lose heart in this season of waiting for what's next. Start a small group at church. Can you dance? Volunteer to start teaching every week at the community center. Do you have the gift of encouragement? Visit a nursing home. And take the time you need to get to know Jesus more and more. Because if you do, when it's time to take your next steps, the path will be as clear as day.

Nº. 37

GETTING STRONGER

"Fear not, for I am with you; be not dismayed, for I am your God; I will strengthen you, I will help you, I will uphold you with my righteous right hand."

ISAIAH 41:10

Have you ever chosen a word for the year? Maybe the word relates to something you want to accomplish or work on. One year I chose the word *strong* as my word for the year. And I was able to use it for many different areas in my life—becoming stronger physically, becoming stronger in my relationships, becoming stronger in my work, faith, and more. Whenever you're being restored or you're in a new season of life, you need to work on gaining strength.

Romans 5:3–5 says, "We rejoice in our sufferings, knowing that suffering produces endurance, and endurance produces character, and character produces hope, and hope does not put us to shame, because God's love has been poured into our hearts through the Holy Spirit who has been given to us." Every time you face challenges, friend, go back to this verse and the one above from Isaiah. Let them both be reminders to you that God is in the midst of whatever you're facing! You can come out stronger than when you went into the battle. Rather than questioning God about why He's doing what He's doing, *trust the process.* As your faith roots grow deeper and stronger, the storms that come will be easier to withstand. Everything is easier when you have strength!

Embrace Your New

Isn't it amazing that we can actually draw from God's strength? God is our Source of strength, and He lends it to us in our daily lives as well as during times of weakness, difficulty, and transition. It's so easy to forget that strength doesn't come from us; it doesn't come from what we can muster up on our own. Isaiah 40:31 (NIV) says, "Those who hope in the LORD will renew their strength. They will soar on wings like eagles; they will run and not grow weary, they will walk and not be faint." When we don't have to find the strength to face each day, our strength comes from our hope in God. What a gift!

N°. 38

LOVING YOURSELF

For no one ever hated his own flesh,
but nourishes and cherishes it,
just as Christ does the church.
EPHESIANS 5:29

We can get down on ourselves when things don't happen the way we wanted them to. When things don't go your way, ask yourself this question: *Do I love myself?* One way to know if you truly love yourself is by reading the definition of *love*. First Corinthians 13:4–8 says, "Love is patient and kind; love does not envy or boast; it is not arrogant or rude. It does not insist on its own way; it is not irritable or resentful; it does not rejoice at wrongdoing, but rejoices with the truth. Love bears all things, believes all things, hopes all things, endures all things. Love never ends."

We often hear these verses read at weddings, but what if we took these principles and applied them to how we treat ourselves? Are you patient and kind to yourself? Do you embrace your own uniqueness and avoid comparing yourself to others? Do you recognize your value without needing applause from others? Do you know that you are worthy because of God's love for you? It really makes you think, doesn't it? A part of becoming new is loving yourself—the *you* that you really are. The *you* that God created and knit in your mother's womb. *You*—flaws and all.

Embrace Your New

This week, write down each negative thought you have about yourself. Then, next to each–write a positive truth about yourself. I want you to write something happy or good or joyful about yourself. Learn to build yourself up instead of tearing yourself down. I'll go first. As I look at my stomach, I realize it will never look the same as it did before I had kids. The truth: I gave birth, which is a blessing, and my body was able to be a home for my babies. Now, as you start to call yourself anything negative or think anything bad about yourself, flip it in your mind. Be grateful for who you are and truly love the beautiful person God created you to be. You can walk up to the mirror now and tell that beautiful person you see in the reflection, I love you.

N°. 39

THE HEART

But the Lord said to Samuel, "Do not look on his appearance or on the height of his stature, because I have rejected him. For the Lord sees not as man sees: man looks on the outward appearance, but the Lord looks on the heart."

I SAMUEL 16:7

There are many passages in the Bible about how God is particularly interested in our hearts, meaning the deeper, internal aspects of who we are—our thoughts, desires, motives, and affections.

Here are just a few of them:

"Create in me a clean heart, O God, and renew a right spirit within me" (Psalm 51:10).

"As in water face reflects face, so the heart of man reflects the man" (Proverbs 27:19).

"A glad heart makes a cheerful face, but by sorrow of heart the spirit is crushed" (Proverbs 15:13).

"Blessed are the pure in heart, for they shall see God" (Matthew 5:8).

"The good person out of the good treasure of his heart produces good, and the evil person out of his evil treasure produces evil, for out of the abundance of the heart his mouth speaks" (Luke 6:45).

After reading these passages, which one stood out to you most? It's important to know that purity of heart, from a biblical perspective, is not about sinless perfection; it's about having a heart that is genuinely devoted to God, seeking righteousness, and being transformed. Take a look inside and ask yourself, *Is my heart pure*? If the answer is *no*, then what's holding you back from living a Christ-centered life, one where you are able to live in freedom, knowing that He is for you and wants to take care of you? Friend, allow Him to heal your heart today.

Embrace Your New

Let's pray together: Lord, You know my heart. I pray that You will cleanse me of any impurities that are keeping me from having a loving relationship with You. Help me to change my ways and for my heart to be healed, as You are my Creator, my Restorer, and my Redeemer. In Jesus' name I pray, amen.

Nº. 40

FINDING YOUR VOICE

I have been crucified with Christ.
It is no longer I who live,
but Christ who lives in me.
And the life I now live in the flesh I live
by faith in the Son of God,
who loved me and gave himself for me.
GALATIANS 2:20

Your voice matters! Remember, Christ lives in you, so when you speak, you are allowing God to speak through you. This is no small thing. Many times, people pleasers, like me, feel as if speaking up is rude, so we choose not to say anything. But that's not the case. You are not only worthy enough to speak up, but you can speak with conviction. You are free from living according to everyone else's standards. Jesus loves you so much He died for you. You don't have to prove yourself or seek validation from outside sources. Your voice matters because you are loved and accepted by the Creator of the universe.

From today on, as you go about life, speak up, knowing that what you have to say is important. If you are not speaking up, there is love that is not being expressed, there is hope that is not being shared, and there is truth that is being silenced. Remember, you were given unique callings and gifts that only you can bring to the world. It could be that someone is just waiting for you to speak so they can experience His love for the first time. So the next time you feel the urge, say it, do it, and experience the goodness of God.

Embrace Your New

Let's look at an example of finding your voice. Say you don't want to go to a party, but you're worried about what others will think if you don't go. You can simply listen to your heart (because all things flow from it) and what God has placed on it. If your heart is telling you not to go, it's okay to say: "Thank you so much for the invitation, but I won't be able to attend. I hope you have a great time!" and leave it at that. You don't have to make up an excuse or find one; just being thankful, truthful, and direct is enough. Try this the next time you're tempted to keep the peace. Find your voice!

your word is

and a ligh

Psal

ump to my feet

o my path.

9:105

N°. 41

THINGS TAKE TIME

But do not overlook this one fact, beloved, that with the Lord one day is as a thousand years, and a thousand years as one day.

II PETER 3:8

Being restored takes time. We often want a quick fix or "five quick steps to a better you," but healing, forgiving, and changing our outlook and mindset can *take time*. Don't be too hard on yourself if you're getting frustrated by how long it's taking. Trust me—it has been hard for me too! Often, when we're used to thinking a certain way, change can be easier said than done. Consistency and time are key in this process.

Second Peter 3:8 reminds us that God is in and through everything. He knew you before you were even born! He wants you to trust in Him and have *patience* in what He's doing. And who better to trust than the Lord? It can be hard for us to understand this, but God sees it much differently than we do. We need to be okay not knowing how long things will take or when things will happen—or even *if* they will happen! I'm sure you can look back on your younger years and wonder how everything happened so fast. Each day seemed the same as the last, but all of a sudden, that season of your life has passed. So, friend, enjoy the season you're in. Soak up all you can where you are now and enjoy each and every day that you wake up with breath in your lungs. That is a blessing. Don't wish this time or day away for what's next, but rather soak it in, remember that all things take time, and enjoy what God has in store for you.

Embrace Your New

When you find yourself wishing the day away or wanting to be in the next season of life, come back to this devotion. Remind yourself to enjoy where you are, when you are, and lean on the Lord. Pray for guidance and for the Lord to be with you as you take each day one at a time. I pray you will enjoy where you are as you realize that God has you there for a reason.

N°. 42

THE LIGHT

Jesus spoke to them, saying,
"I am the light of the world.
Whoever follows me will not walk in darkness,
but will have the light of life."
JOHN 8:12

Recently, I was watering my plants, and God had me notice something. My daughter and I had saved pumpkin seeds from last year's carving pumpkins we'd bought at the store, and we decided to plant our own pumpkins this year. We put them in the ground in different places—some where there's more sunlight than others. I watered them equally . . . and now that they are starting to grow, can you guess which ones are growing more than the others? The ones in the sunlight.

Psalm 119:105 says: "Your word is a lamp to my feet and a light to my path." Jesus is the light of the world, and the Word of the Lord lights our paths. I love how God can give us reminders of Himself that reflect His Word—even through nature. We need to live in the light, just like the plants, in order to grow in our faith and to know what direction to go. If we are in the darkness, or without much light, we simply will not grow in our faith, just like those pumpkin plants. They're existing . . .

but they're not thriving like those that were planted in full sunlight.

Second Corinthians 4:6 says, "For God, who said, 'Let light shine out of darkness,' has shone in our hearts to give the light of the knowledge of the glory of God in the face of Jesus Christ." Even as we look inward, is the light shining in our hearts? Or has it dimmed? Psalm 18:28 says: "For it is you who light my lamp; the Lord my God lightens my darkness." We are being made new and restored as we turn toward the light.

Embrace Your New

Allow the Light of the World to shine upon you, as you turn toward God and away from your past. Soak up His light so that you may also be a light to others and help guide their way toward everlasting life through Jesus. It is a beautiful thing to share your testimony with others! You can be a light to others by shining the light of the Lord that's within you on others. As you plant your own gardens or close your eyes in the sunshine, be reminded that Jesus is the light of the world—and whoever follows Him will have the light of life!

N°. 43

GRASS ISN'T ALWAYS GREENER

The Lord is good to those who wait for him,
to the soul who seeks him.
LAMENTATIONS 3:25

When we look at where we are now in life, it's tempting to think, *Wow—what if I'd taken that other job?* or, *What if I had done this instead . . . ?* The thing is, God worked it out, and you are right *where you need to be*. You did what you were supposed to do—because He's working in and *through it all*. There is no use trying to reconstruct the situations you've been in or redo the things you think you should have said or done differently. Don't be so hard on yourself. Rather, trust in the Lord to guide your path.

Even when I was down about not finding my husband earlier in life, I can take comfort in the fact that God was working in it. He had to prepare my husband for me, in His timing, not in my timing. If we'd met earlier, maybe it wouldn't have worked out. Obsessing about the what-ifs in life can steal the joy from the story God has lovingly prepared for us. He wants us to live in the present and in peace and be joyful, knowing that the grass isn't always greener, and to lean on Him in full faith and trust, rather than on your own understanding.

Embrace Your New

As you are on the path of being restored, consider your thoughts about your life. Do you ever wish things had happened differently or wonder if the grass really would have been greener on the other side? Do you ever look up your exes or that crush you had in middle school to see where they ended up and imagine what your life would be like if you were with them? Do you pass by the place where you were offered a job yet turned it down and wonder, What if? *As humans, we love to wonder about these things, but it's better to be grateful for the life God has so graciously given to us—messiness and all. Remember, the Lord is good to those who wait for Him—seek Him first.*

Nº. 44

THOUGHTS OF OTHERS

"As you wish that others would do to you, do so to them."
LUKE 6:31

As we lean into how we think about ourselves, we should also consider what we think others think of us. We may imagine that others in our lives—or even those who pass by us on the street—think certain negative things about us. Let's break it down.

First, we don't know the thoughts of others. We can project our own negative thoughts and insecurities onto what we imagine others think about us, but that's not always true. When we do this, we only continue to put ourselves down. And do we deserve to be put down? No! As Luke 6:31 says, whatever you wish that others would do to you, do it to them. Do you wish that others thought negatively about themselves? Of course not! What if you heard someone say, "Well, I thought you may think this about me . . ." You would probably think, *Wow—I would never think that!*

Second, doing this only hurts our feelings about the

other person. These thoughts we have projected onto someone else may not even be true, but they can create a divide between ourselves and that person.

Third, the more we do this, the more we can believe these false thoughts about ourselves. We are to remember who we are and Whose we are!

Lastly, be reminded we are all God's creation—we're all created uniquely. Let's end today's reading with a helpful reminder from Philippians 4:8: "Finally, brothers, whatever is true, whatever is honorable, whatever is just, whatever is pure, whatever is lovely, whatever is commendable, if there is any excellence, if there is anything worthy of praise, think about these things."

Embrace Your New

Friend, next time you imagine that someone is thinking about you negatively, stop yourself and remember this devotion. Also, be reminded of what you read in Philippians 4:8: Think of positive things, not negative things. Replace those negative thoughts with lovely, pure, commendable, joyful thoughts, and honor yourself. Don't work for the praise of others, but rather, know that you are already loved and are worthy.

Nº. 45

BE JOYFUL

May the words of my mouth and the meditation
of my heart be pleasing in your sight,
Lord, my Rock and my Redeemer.

PSALM 19:14 NIV

You can decide to wake up and focus on all the bad things in your life, overanalyzing how to fix them all (guilty here!), or you can look to David, who wrote Psalm 19:14, as a model for prayer and reflection. In this verse, David asks God to help his words and thoughts to be pleasing to God. This means filtering out any negative or discouraging thoughts and replacing them with God's goodness, faithfulness, and power. Having thoughts of bitterness, jealousy, or revenge? Think about God's grace and seek peace. Are you frustrated about the situation at hand? Think about the people you love, the beauty of creation, or that flower you saw blooming through the crack of the sidewalk. Are you criticizing others in your mind? Think about some of their good attributes.

No matter what negative situation you find yourself in, try to press the pause button. Close your eyes and try to think of five ways you can see God in that moment. Where can you see the Light (Jesus!)? When you see the Light, don't let it go;

hold on to it. Safeguard your happiness by keeping your eyes on the Light.

If you're having a hard time finding joy, remember Romans 12:12. It says, "Rejoice in hope, be patient in tribulation, be constant in prayer." Ask for God to reveal what is stealing your joy and ask Him to help restore you in this process you are in, friend. Remember, He's always there, and it's always in His timing. It can take practice to find that joy and be happy, but God will help you get there.

Embrace Your New

Proverbs 17:22 reminds us: "A joyful heart is good medicine, but a crushed spirit dries up the bones." If it's hard for you to find joy, turn on some worship music. Listen to the words, and be reminded that God loves you! There will be sad days and happy days, but God wants you to live out of the abundance of joy that only He can give! Whatever is weighing on your heart, darkening that light inside you, bring it to God and let Him take it, so that your thoughts and words will be filled with His peace and joy.

N°. 46

RESTORING YOUR FAITH

Jesus said to him, "I am the way,
and the truth, and the life.
No one comes to the Father except through me."
JOHN 14:6

Have you lost some of your faith throughout life? John 14:6 says Jesus is the way, the truth, and the life. Do you have a hard time believing this sometimes? Sometimes our faith can be shattered when we feel we've lost trust in God or that He's forgotten us. It's easy to push God aside and take our own path. Before you get too far down that road, though, you should know that God is patient with our doubts. Your doubts do not frighten or offend Him. Pray about them (even if you don't feel like it). Ask God for the evidence and reassurance you need to trust Him again. Doubt doesn't mean you have no faith—in fact, your doubts may be just the pathway for God's grace and power to work through you.

The process of restoring your faith can take time, but being a Christian doesn't mean we automatically have an easy life—we were never promised that. During this season, try to remember that nothing can separate you from God's love (Romans 8:38–39). Remember all the ways God has been faithful to you in the past. Remember that God works through *all things* (even your doubts) to bring about His will. As you walk through this process, keep leaning into God. Address your doubts, be honest about them, pray about them, and reach out to trusted friends about what you are feeling. It could be that God will use this time in your life to give you a deeper understanding of who He is. And you'll want to be paying attention for that.

Embrace Your New

There are so many ways to build your faith! Reading the Bible, singing and listening to worship music, joining a church, journaling, being out in nature, and finding a small group are just some ways to help restore your faith. Having a relationship with the Lord is so important to your faith. You can pray anytime, anywhere, about anything, and God will always listen.

N°. 47

CARRYING THE WEIGHT

Anxiety in a man's heart weighs him down,

but a good word makes him glad.

PROVERBS 12:25

When we carry the burden of our past pain, it can weigh us down. So much so that we can sometimes physically feel the weight on our chest. Picture two scales—one side is full of sand and maybe it can bear no more weight. The other side is free, ready to receive. As you empty the sand from your side, Jesus is there, taking it all on. When this happens, you can feel this weight lifted off your chest, maybe even literally.

Part of restoration is relying on faith over feelings. A lot of us feel like we have to carry the weight, that it's a part of us. Like a ball and chain constantly tied to us, we drag that weight around, and it steals our joy. But friend, what a gift that we have Jesus. He is our Redeemer, our joy, our salvation, our life. He is life-giving, and He can *restore your soul*. He can take those burdens and all that weighs you down.

It's up to you to release that weight. It can be hard to do this, especially if it's been around for a while. But friend, pray for that *release*, and pray for God to help guide you in those next steps. Sometimes that's saying "yes" to a new direction, or maybe it's stepping away from something that's no longer serving you. It can be uncomfortable, but that's where faith over fear comes in. It will be for good, and for His glory. God may ask you to say "no" to some things to help release that weight and bring you freedom. Whatever it is, act on those nudges, and release all you've been carrying.

Embrace Your New

Giving up control is hard. Doing something new—even something that's good for you—can be hard. But once you start this practice of letting God lead and giving Him what's weighing on you, you will feel lighter. The light will be able to shine through to you, and you will learn to deepen your faith and lessen the worry you have in life. God wants us to be happy, and He's here to take on those burdens we endure. He's got you, friend!

N°. 48

OTHERS' BURDENS

Bear one another's burdens,
and so fulfill the law of Christ.
GALATIANS 6:2

My son's friend broke a bone at the start of his summer break. When we saw his sling, we knew this young boy was going to have a tough summer. A broken bone is a burden we can see, as we immediately notice the sling or cast. However, you can't see someone's insides when they're broken and trying to heal. This passage in Galatians is a beautiful example to live by—to be there for others, to be in community, and to connect with and help one another. Be available to let others pour out what's in their souls. But as you help them, know that you don't have to carry that emotional weight around with you. Rather, you can lift it up to the Father. As you're there for your friend, family member, or neighbor, you can lend a helping hand or a listening ear. If you are a parent, you can be there for your children and create a safe space for them to share what's on their hearts. I'm always one to offer advice, but sometimes people—especially kids—just want a listening ear and a safe person with whom they can share their innermost thoughts. Friend, this is a great reminder not to place what's weighing your heart down on young ears. It's not up to a young person or a sensitive individual to be able to help carry that emotional weight. As we learn what others are going through, we can help by encouraging them to join a support group, talk to a therapist or pastor, or get professional help.

Embrace Your New

Every person's burdens are unique. Some are deeper than others, and some are longer lasting than others. But no matter what the struggle is, we were created for community; we were never meant to walk this journey alone. We can't always see when someone is hurting, so make sure to check in with others and create a safe place for them to share without judgment, letting them know that what they say is safe with you. We all have burdens to bear, and being vulnerable is hard. As you find community, you will feel safe sharing with others and being there for them.

Nº. 49

PRAISING THROUGH IT

For we walk by faith, not by sight.

II CORINTHIANS 5:7

Have you ever done a trust fall? You stand with someone behind you who is ready to catch you, but if you stumble before you're caught, you demonstrate that you no longer trust that person to catch you. Well, friend, where are you with your faith? If Jesus were standing behind you, would you feel like He's going to catch you, or would you take a step back during your fall to attempt to catch yourself?

Friend, you can trust in Him! Today, be honest with yourself about your faith, and know that He is a Waymaker—for His plans, not yours. Jesus is your Redeemer, your Deliverer—He is your life! As you go through a broken season, choose to praise Him through it. Keep your eyes on Him rather than on your situation. We often only praise God when happy times come and only pray when the hard times come. What if we changed things up to praise Him in the storms and pray to Him in the sunshine? Pray and praise during *all* seasons.

As your relationship with God deepens, you will grow

those faith roots and become closer to Him. He wants a relationship with you, and He wants you to rely on Him fully. He provides you with forgiveness when you deserve to fall. He is a Waymaker, and He can surround you with love and peace, even when it makes no sense. Let yourself be covered in peace rather than by pain. He can give you so much grace, no matter how broken you may feel. You may not feel like praising Him, but friend, turn on some worship music, pour out your heart, and let Him replace your pain with peace.

Embrace Your New

Friend, know that God can move mountains as you worship and praise Him in both the storms and the sunshine! The mountains may not be moved in your timing, but they will be moved according to His plan. Align your heart with God's and learn to rely on your faith rather than wanting to take control of things yourself. And remember to both pray and praise—no matter what is happening around you!

N°. 50

FEELING LOVE

We love because he first loved us.

I JOHN 4:19

Friend, Jesus loves you. As you are becoming made new, you need to feel loved and cared for through the process. If you feel love by receiving physical touch like hugs, you can close your eyes and picture Jesus holding out His hand to you or giving you a warm embrace. If you like to receive gifts, accept the gift of salvation from your Lord and Savior and the gift of Him always being there for you. If your love language is quality time, spend special moments with God. Dive into the Word, reading a devotional or journal, turn on worship music, and come to Him in prayer. If you love words of affirmation, the Bible is full of God's love for you! Find a few favorite verses to memorize today to be reminded of how much He loves you. If you like having acts of service performed for you, remember that Jesus died on the cross for you. John 3:16 reminds us: "For God so loved the world, that he gave his only Son, that whoever believes in him should not perish but have eternal life." What a beautiful act of service and a gift all in one!

First John 4:16 says, "So we have come to know and to believe the love that God has for us. God is love, and whoever abides in love abides in God, and God abides in him." What a beautiful reminder that as you become made new in the Lord, you can feel loved by Him!

Embrace Your New

Thinking of the wonderful variety of ways we can feel loved can be a beautiful reminder. Sometimes we do feel forgotten or unloved, but I want you to push that negativity away and replace it with the truth! It can be easier to go back to how we were than to be made new, but I challenge you to accept the love that is given to you. In order to feel the best love of all–God's love–you simply need to be a child of God and believe in your Savior. You are loved, friend!

Commit your work
to the LORD,
and your plans
will be established.
Proverbs 16:3

Nº. 51

LOVING OTHERS

Beloved, let us love one another, for love is from God, and whoever loves has been born of God and knows God.

I JOHN 4:7

Knowing how to best express love to our friends, family members, coworkers, and other people in our lives can brighten things up for everyone. Have you ever known someone who lights up when you do a task for them? They like acts of service. Have you ever told someone they did a great job at work and they got the biggest smile on their face? Their love language is most likely words of affirmation. Have you ever hugged a little one and they kept holding on or asked for more cuddles? They probably love physical touch. Have you ever given a friend a gift and they were so touched? Their love language could very well be receiving gifts. Have you ever gone on a date night and your significant other wished it would never end? Their love language is probably quality time. Another hint for figuring out someone's love language is noticing how they show their love to others. There's a good chance that's how they like to receive love too!

It's so great to know that we are all made different, yet we're all made in the image of God. As we discover how best to love others, our relationships become stronger. If someone you care about is unsure of their love language, try different things to determine what it is. Write a card to tell them how special they are, give them a hug, pick up their favorite snack at the store, spend extra time with them, or complete a project for them. See what lights them up the most—then keep showing them love!

Embrace Your New

Friend, remember that love is from God. He loved us first! We can go about life feeling unloved when our needs are unmet, but it's important to find our voice and communicate our love language to others, then ask what makes them *feel loved and happy and cared for. Let Jesus' light shine through you as you love others and experience love yourself. John 15:12 is a beautiful reminder of this: "This is my commandment, that you love one another as I have loved you."*

Nº. 52

FOR THE LORD

Whatever you do, work heartily,
as for the Lord and not for men.
COLOSSIANS 3:23

Let's start off today's devotion with a prayer: *Lord, thank You for this reminder in Colossians to maintain a fresh view of life and know that I am not working for anyone but You. Whether I'm at home or at work, help me to remember that all that I do is for You and for Your glory. In Jesus' name, amen.*

Think about the work you do, whether at home or at your job, and ask yourself, *Do I ever feel like I'm doing this work for God?* It's a beautiful thing to know that God has so many wonderful purposes for you, that He has created you to be great at what you're great at. He has put you where you are—where you need to be—for a reason. Some days at work or at home can be rough. But when you have this perspective—that you are working for the Lord—you do what you need to do with an open heart and for a greater purpose. You can see God working in and through you to fulfill His purposes for you as you complete your tasks each day.

Here are two more great reminders from Scripture:

"Commit your work to the Lord, and your plans will be established" (Proverbs 16:3). And, "Let the favor of the Lord our God be upon us, and establish the work of our hands upon us; yes, establish the work of our hands!" (Psalm 90:17).

Embrace Your New

Think about all the things you do in life. Going back to Colossians 3:23 can remind you that you're doing everything—whether at work, at home, or anywhere else—for the Lord. He has a greater plan for it all, and we are here for Him, just as He is here for us. It's all about Him. It's all about His glory and His plans, more than ours. It can be hard to put that into perspective, but as you change the way you view things, you can have a renewed outlook on the things you do, which makes it easier for you to do them with all your heart and for the Lord.

Nº. 53

I GET TO DO THIS

I know that you can do all things,
and that no purpose of yours
can be thwarted.

JOB 42:2

As we dive a little deeper into thinking about all the things we do, let's talk about the part of us that tends to complain when we *have* to do certain things. I don't know about you, but I hate cleaning the shower. It's my least-favorite thing to do. There are also days when it feels like my kids all need me at once, and it's challenging to keep up with it all. Then there are the days when the laundry pile is a mile high, or I have way too much on my to-do list, or I have to juggle multiple responsibilities and projects at work . . . Life can get so overwhelming at times!

I'm sure you've been there too, friend. You also have days where it's a lot, when you can't seem to find any peace in the chaos. But I have a wonderful five-word phrase I want you to repeat to yourself in these moments . . . are you ready? Here it is: *I get to do this*. Wow! I *get* to. Maybe you're in a season right now that you prayed for years ago (I am!), and now that you're here, it's not all sunshine and rainbows. There are good days and hard days, but that's okay! In the hard moments, repeat to yourself: *I get to do this.* Then remind yourself that what you get to do is what God wants you to do—and it's wonderful.

Embrace Your New

When you find yourself complaining that the house isn't as clean as you wish, tell yourself that you have a house and that is a blessing. When you feel frustrated with your kids, remind yourself that you have kids and they are a blessing. When difficult days at work make you want to pull your hair out, tell yourself that you have a job and it is a blessing. The list can go on and on. Friend, this is a good time to be reminded of the words of Ephesians 2:10: "For we are his workmanship, created in Christ Jesus for good works, which God prepared beforehand." God knew you before you were even born, and you have so many wonderful purposes. When you're tempted to complain about what God has set before you in your life, tell yourself: I get to do this!

Nº. 54

NOT BY WORKS

For by grace you have been saved through faith.
And this is not your own doing;
it is the gift of God, not a result of works,
so that no one may boast.
EPHESIANS 2:8–9

Sometimes we feel like we aren't "good" Christians. We feel like everyone at church does a better job at being a Christian than we do, and we think we need to do more to be enough for God. But the truth is, there is no "point system" with God. You don't get points for going to church or for bringing a neighbor a meal. You don't get points for serving others or lose points when you fail. God is full of grace. It's by His mercy that we are saved. His grace is not something we have to earn; we just have to receive Jesus as our Savior and be born again.

It's important to note that God's work of restoration in us is not achieved through human effort or good deeds either. This process will be achieved through God's grace and our faith in Jesus Christ. Just like it is with our salvation, there is nothing we can *do* that will bring about the transformation and healing God offers us. Sure, we can pray and grow deeper in our faith and serve others—good works are a fruit of the transformation that God brings. But external actions, such as volunteering at the food pantry, are not going to speed up this process or bring it to completion. God's restoration happens at the heart level. And only God can restore our hearts, heal our wounds, and renew our minds. Isn't this a comforting truth? This means we don't have to perform. It's our job to trust God with all our doubts and fears, then let Him do His work in us.

Embrace Your New

Friend, restoration is not about trying harder to be good or making up for past mistakes; it's about resting in the finished work of Jesus. It sounds easy, but keep in mind that God's goal is a complete transformation that impacts who we are at the deepest level. There will, no doubt, be hard situations to face and thought processes to be challenged, but when we come out on the other side, we will be stronger in every way imaginable.

N°. 55

REPENTING

Repent therefore, and turn back,
that your sins may be blotted out,
that times of refreshing may come
from the presence of the Lord.
ACTS 3:19–20

When you hear the word *repent*, does it make you feel nervous? It's a strong word, but friend, if we are honest, God already knows what we have done, and He knows how our hearts feel about it. Repenting allows us to be released of this sin, and it's a beautiful thing because it gives us a pure heart. Romans 6:14 reminds us: "For sin will have no dominion over you, since you are not under law but under grace." You are not alone, friend. We all have fallen short, and all of us have sinned: "For all have sinned and fall short of the glory of God" (Romans 3:23). This is so true! We hear about this in Romans 6:23, as well: "For the wages of sin is death, but the free gift of God is eternal life in Christ Jesus our Lord." For God, it's all about what's in our hearts.

When you look at where you have fallen short, what comes to mind? The great thing is that no matter what it is, you can come to God, anytime, talk to Him about it, and repent.

He wants to hear from you! As you become restored, you may realize you have past sins that have been buried deep down. When they come to the surface, it can be hard to deal with. But when you choose to repent, you are able to turn your back on these sins and receive the gift of forgiveness from God. And you don't have to wait for this opportunity! In the words of Acts 22:16, you can "rise and be baptized and wash away your sins, calling on his name."

Embrace Your New

Repenting isn't easy, but being real with God, coming to Him with a pure heart, and asking for His forgiveness will help cleanse your soul of whatever has been weighing it down, whether it's from today or from many yesterdays ago. You are loved, and can be seen as blameless in front of God, because Jesus died for your sins. Receive this gift today!

Nº. 56

RESTORING YOUR SOUL

He restores my soul.
He leads me in paths of righteousness
for his name's sake.
PSALM 23:3

Where can you find God in the storm? The Bible tells us that God is especially near to the brokenhearted (Psalm 34:18). He doesn't stand apart from our struggles, watching from a distance; He enters into them with us and leads us on the right path, for His name's sake! He restores our souls. He cleanses us of all the hurts and pains we carry. We just need to hand it all over to Him. But how can we "give it to God" and simply walk away—especially when we believed for so long that we had it all under control? The truth is, giving it over to God is an ongoing act of surrender. It's a daily choice to trust, pray, release control, and rest in His peace. If we're not careful, we can give it to God one minute and then pick it back up the next. The next time you feel the urge to pick it back up, think about your limits; recognize God's infinite power, wisdom, and love; and leave the storm with Him.

Surrendering to God and giving Him all your worries and concerns will give you a peace beyond understanding. But rest assured—the house will never be fully cleaned, your life will never be perfect, and more storms will come. When you find yourself in a new moment with new worries and concerns, you'll need to go through all the steps again—trust, pray, release control, and rest. And if you start to pick it back up, compare your limitations to God's and then walk away.

Embrace Your New

Friend, I pray you can join me in releasing to God whatever's stealing *your joy today. Write down what is on your heart—all the things that are weighing you down—then assign those things to Him. Whether it's an act of visualizing you giving it over to Him or writing down on paper the reminder that God's got this and then crossing it off your list, you can do it! When anxiety pops up or you start to fall back into the norm of trying to fix everything, find five ways you feel blessed or can see God through in the midst of the challenge, and let your soul be restored.*

N°. 57

YOUR THOUGHTS

Do not be conformed to this world,
but be transformed by the renewal of your mind,
that by testing you may discern what is the will of God,
what is good and acceptable and perfect.
ROMANS 12:2

What goes through your mind on an average day? Are you putting yourself down? Do you worry about what everyone else thinks? Are you thinking you're not worthy of good things? It's so easy to allow false statements to fill our minds. But how do we decide what is false and what is true? And how can we push false beliefs out of our minds?

You can start by comparing your thoughts with what the Bible says. If a thought is contrary to Scripture, then it is a false belief. For instance, if you are thinking, *I'm not worthy of joy*, remember that in John 15:11 (NIV), Jesus said, "I have told you this so that my joy may be in you and that your joy may be complete." Then you will recognize that your thought is false. Also, ask yourself, *Where did this belief come from?* Was it influenced by your culture or a past trauma? Once you find the origin of the thought, you may be better able to access its validity.

Now let's put these false beliefs behind you and allow the Lord to renew your mind. Memorizing Scripture is key. As soon as a false belief enters your head, speak Scripture to it. If your thought is, *I am worthless*, respond with the words of God: "You are precious in My sight" (Isaiah 43:4 CSB). If your thought is, *I hate what I did*, respond with: "There is therefore now no condemnation for those who are in Christ Jesus" (Romans 8:1). You'll find that false beliefs disappear when you speak God's Word. What about those intrusive thoughts that won't leave? Try singing worship songs about God's greatness. This will help you put all other thoughts to the side.

Know this: You don't have to let your thoughts run wild. Capture them in their tracks and live a more peaceful life through Jesus.

Embrace Your New

Let's pray: Lord, help me to take my thoughts captive. Please take away whatever is stealing my joy. Help me to replace any untruths with truth and to give myself grace. Lord, I pray for peace of mind. In Jesus' name, amen.

Nº. 58

OVERCOMING THE WORLD

For everyone who has been
born of God overcomes the world.
And this is the victory that has
overcome the world—our faith.
I JOHN 5:4

We can get so worked up inside about things that we have no control over and fixate on problems or situations that really just live in our minds. Often, if we are a product of trauma that took place in the past, we can become hypervigilant of what's around us and allow anxiety, fear, and worry to run our lives. The great news is that if this describes you, friend, you aren't alone. Instead of ignoring or suppressing these feelings, you can rationalize them by bringing them into the light of God's truth (just like you did with your thoughts in the previous devotion). Acknowledge your fear and compare it to God's Word. For instance, if you have a fear of failing in an area of your life, whether that be in your career or in your relationships, remind yourself of Romans 8:28 (NIV): "All things God works for the good of those who love Him."

Or maybe you have fears about the future: *What will happen? How will things will unfold?* Remind yourself of Jesus' words in Matthew 6:34 (NIV): "Do not worry about tomorrow, for tomorrow will worry about itself. Each day has enough trouble of its own."

When we replace our worldly fears with God's truth, we learn to calm our hearts and focus on the present—what's in front of us and what's actually true—rather than jumping to wild conclusions. We can find peace in prayer and in taking a few deep, cleansing breaths. Our faith can overcome any fear. We can sit with Jesus, for we are never alone . . . He's always with us. In those times when we can't see what's ahead, know that He's already been there. God transcends time, and He has overcome the world.

Embrace Your New

When anxiety starts to take over your life, it becomes all-consuming. At first, there's a little muscle tension, then you start thinking the worst, and before you know it, you're losing sleep. When this happens, it's important to pursue peace. Surrender it all to God on a daily (or hourly) basis, meditate on Scripture, go for a walk with a mentor, or get some rest. Remember, you can find peace in His presence, as He is with you each day.

N°. 59

PRAYER

Pray without ceasing.

I THESSALONIANS 5:17

How is your prayer life? Do you pray? Do you pray when you or someone else is having an issue? Do you give thanks to God in the good times? Today, consider how you pray. Prayer is one of the best ways of building your relationship with God. Romans 12:12 says: "Rejoice in hope, be patient in tribulation, be constant in prayer." Read that a few times over and let it sink in. We're called to pray at all times, being steadfast in prayer, letting God know our requests, while praying for one another and knowing that He hears us.

You can come to Him in prayer anytime, anywhere, and for anything. You can come to Him with whatever's on your heart—in praise or for whatever is weighing your heart down.

You can talk to God when you're driving or in the shower . . . just pour your heart out like you're talking to a friend. The great thing is, He already knows you, friend—your mess, your joys, your sadness, your hope—everything. He is your heavenly Father, who walks beside you each day. Just as a child lets their parents lead them, you can let the Lord direct you. He wants to take your anxieties and worries away, and they're in safe hands with Him. Go to Him in prayer, then let Him work through your circumstances and bring you into a place of joy and peace.

The more we pray, the stronger our connection with God becomes, and our hearts grow to be more aligned with His. This helps us to hear better from Him and obey those nudges. Our relationship with Him becomes stronger, and we can have the peace that surpasses all understanding throughout all types of trials.

Embrace Your New

Dive deeper into prayer this week. Try something new in your prayer life. That could look like adding praise into your prayers, talking to God as you would chat with a friend, or even starting a nightly prayer routine. As you pray, think about those for whom you can pray who aren't on your normal list. Maybe it's someone you passed by on the street today or a friend who hasn't been that nice to you lately. Whoever it is, come to God with them in mind, and let Him work in and through their lives. Today, find peace in prayer and release it all to Him.

N°. 60

REST IN RESTORATION

"Come to me, all who labor and are heavy laden, and I will give you rest. Take my yoke upon you, and learn from me, for I am gentle and lowly in heart, and you will find rest for your souls. For my yoke is easy, and my burden is light."

MATTHEW 11:28-30

Do you find it hard to rest? You may have so much going on in your life—between home, work, relationships, family, friends, and more—that finding time to actually rest isn't something you have room for on your to-do list. You may even feel like you can't take a moment to yourself in the middle of a busy day (guilty here!). As we look at the seasons and how they change, we can observe that nature takes a rest. Think of the bears that hibernate or the plants that go dormant until the next season. In His creation, God allows rest. Even as we sleep at night, our bodies grow and repair tissue, allowing healing and restoration to take place. Jeremiah 31:25 says, "For I will satisfy the weary soul, and every languishing soul I will replenish."

Friend, do you have a weary soul? If so, you may need to quiet your mind and let peace and truth replace any brokenness as you allow yourself to be made new and restored. Friend, you are allowed to rest without feeling guilty about it. In fact, you are worthy of rest. Take time to sit by the lake and soak in God's beauty all around you, take that walk during your lunch break, or take that much-needed vacation. And remember, it's okay to say "no" to a dinner party when you really just need to relax at home. Allow His rest to restore you.

Embrace Your New

This week, try to find rest and allow peace and calmness into your soul. Replace anxiety, stress, or worry with God's Word and meditate on His love for you. Make time for you—you're allowed to! Even if it's hard for you, embrace rest and welcome it into your life. It can be hard at first, but as you look to your own needs instead of always tending to others, you can know that you, too, are worthy of peace, rest, and joy.

The LORD will fight for you, and you have only to be silent.

Exodus 14:14

N°. 61

SEEING GOD IN IT

"Have I not commanded you?
Be strong and courageous.
Do not be frightened, and do not be dismayed,
for the Lord *your God is with you wherever you go."*
JOSHUA 1:9

I love home-improvement shows. I love seeing the progress from what the house looked like before, through all the mess during the middle phase, and then the final reveal! But when I redid a few of my own homes, I really disliked the middle phase—and all that mess. I remember my living room was covered in dust, and I thought, *Well, I guess it will never look the same again*. But I'm sitting in that living room right now, the dust is all gone, and it looks much different than it did before. The mess was worth it to get to the final reveal.

When we're in the midst of the mess, it's hard to see God through all the dust. But He is with you, wherever you go. He's with you in the mess, in the storms, and in the rain. You can find peace in knowing that you're never alone. You may feel like you're not able to find Him as the rain pours down, but call out His name; He will be by your side. We all go through storms, friend; some of them last for a short bit and others for a long time. It's up to us how we react to the storms . . . will we be steadfast in our faith or easily blown over? We are called to be strong and courageous. We are reminded not to be frightened or dismayed. We can replace our fear with the truth that God is for us—not against us—as we lean on Him and He carries us through the storms.

Embrace Your New

Today, I want you to think of some ways in which you've recently seen God at work in your life and all around you. As you read Joshua 1:9 again, do a faith check. Are you strong and courageous, or are you frightened and dismayed? How can you replace fear with faith and remember that God is with you wherever you go? Today, come to Him in prayer, asking Him to replace any fear you have with faith, then bring whatever is on your heart to Him.

N°. 62

BE STILL

"Be still, and know that I am God."

PSALM 46:10

When you feel like you're in a battle, what do you do? Do you fight back? Do you run away as fast as you can? Do you call up your closest friends and tell them to soldier up? Or do you start building a fortress around yourself? Instinctively, these actions make a lot of sense. However, when you take a look at Scripture, you see the Lord says, "Be still, and know that I am God" (Psalm 46:10). And Exodus 14:14 says: "The Lord will fight for you, and you have only to be silent." While it might not feel right to be still and silent when you are facing difficulties, God reminds us in Scripture that *we don't have to fix it all.* Let's hear that again: We don't have to fix it all. It's not all up to us to figure out, and unless we get that nudge from Him telling us where to go and how to respond, we don't have to step in at all. He is *working* on it and through it all, even when it doesn't make sense to us, and even when it's hard to handle.

During a season of transformation, it may sometimes feel like a battleground. You take two steps forward only to be pushed four steps back. It's common to long for how things used to be, and it's frustrating when whatever is next is taking longer than expected to arrive. But don't lose hope, my friend. You have a connection with the One who can move mountains and part seas. Remember Psalm 62:5 in these times: "For God alone, O my soul, wait in silence, for my hope is from him." Put your trust and hope in the hands of almighty God, and try to be still. Who knows? You could be amazed at what happens next.

Embrace Your New

Practice being still today! Focus your gaze on Him rather than on the problems, situations, anxieties, or worries at hand. Know that there is nothing too big for God to handle. God's power is limitless, all-encompassing, and unmatched by any other force or being. And He wants to take your burdens and replace those thoughts that steal your joy with peace.

No. 63

FRUIT OF THE SPIRIT

The fruit of the Spirit is love, joy, peace, patience, kindness, goodness, faithfulness, gentleness, self-control; against such things there is no law. And those who belong to Christ Jesus have crucified the flesh with its passions and desires.

GALATIANS 5:22–24

As we work on embracing the new, let's take a look at Galatians 5:19–21: "The works of the flesh are evident: sexual immorality, impurity, sensuality, idolatry, sorcery, enmity, strife, jealousy, fits of anger, rivalries, dissensions, divisions, envy, drunkenness, orgies, and things like these. I warn you, as I warned you before, that those who do such things will not inherit the kingdom of God." The next verse lists the different fruit of the Spirit—love, joy, peace, patience, kindness, goodness, faithfulness, gentleness, and self-control. When we accept Jesus as our Lord and Savior, we put to death the desires of the flesh and embrace the fruit of the Spirit.

We live in a broken world, and none of us is perfect. But we can allow God to restore our brokenness and replace it with love, joy, peace, patience, kindness, goodness, faithfulness, gentleness, and self-control. This isn't something that happens overnight, but over time we can gradually change our emotions, responses, and actions. Instead of becoming impatient with our children, we can practice patience. Instead of getting angry about a situation at work, we can take a deep breath and focus on our self-control. Where can you replace the desires of the flesh with the fruit of the Spirit in your life? God will help you!

Embrace Your New

As you become made new and more aware of how the flesh thinks, acts, and responds, you can lean into the fruit of the Spirit in order to live more like Jesus. You can lean into love and find peace and joy when you dive deeper into your faith and walk with the Lord. You can find patience and self-control during stressful times by showing kindness and goodness to yourself and to others. Remain faithful to God and others . . . and remember to be gentle with yourself too. Today, pray to God to help you live out the fruit of the Spirit and open your eyes to where you can make some beautiful changes today.

N°. 64

JUDGING OTHERS

"Judge not, that you be not judged. For with the judgment you pronounce you will be judged, and with the measure you use it will be measured to you. Why do you see the speck that is in your brother's eye, but do not notice the log that is in your own eye? Or how can you say to your brother, 'Let me take the speck out of your eye,' when there is the log in your own eye? You hypocrite, first take the log out of your own eye, and then you will see clearly to take the speck out of your brother's eye."

MATTHEW 7:1-5

Do you ever judge others—how they act, what they look like, how they handled a situation? We've all done it, right? But when we think about it, none of us is perfect. We all have flaws and areas of our lives that we need to work on. In Luke 6:31, Jesus said, "And as you wish that others would do to you, do so to them." Do you ever wish people could see past your flaws or mistakes and see the light inside of you instead?

When you find yourself criticizing others, even in your mind, ask yourself what you find good about them. What positive traits might they have? Can you forgive them for taking your parking spot or cutting in front of you in line?

Matthew 6:14–15 tells us a little more about the importance of forgiveness: "For if you forgive others their trespasses, your heavenly Father will also forgive you, but if you do not forgive others their trespasses, neither will your Father forgive your trespasses." Friend, you don't know that person the way God knows them. If we start to see others as beautiful creatures whom God created, each of them unique, we can stop looking at the world from a judgmental perspective and begin to love and accept others.

Embrace Your New

Friend, we are all different–me, you, the person next door. We all have flaws, and we all have our own struggles. We sometimes tend to judge others rather than forgiving them or finding the good in them. If you find yourself starting to judge, stop. Then tell yourself something good about that person and pray for them. Pray for God to help you see the light, rather than the dark, in others.

Nº. 65

BE OKAY WITH CHANGE

Every good gift and every perfect gift is from above, coming down from the Father of lights, with whom there is no variation or shadow due to change.

JAMES 1:17

With another little one on the way, my husband and I thought it might be time to find a new house with another bedroom. We made a list of everything we'd ever want in a new home—random but unique features, some of which we thought were just a dream. And then one day, to our surprise, we found a house that had it all—except it needed some work. It was an older home, built in the 1800s, and that scared me a little. But God was in it. As we prayed over the house, we gave it up to God. If it was meant to be, it would be ours. We met the couple who bought our old home, and they instantly became some of our best friends. I then knew God had had me redo our home not for us but for them. It took a year for me to feel truly at home in my new (old) house, but in the end, I was okay with change—more than okay, in fact!

As God makes moves in our lives, it can sometimes feel uneasy and uncomfortable, but we have to trust the process—and trust Him. We have to be okay with change and the gifts He gives us, even if we feel hesitant to accept those gifts. The other day my son's knees hurt because of growing pains, and I remember having those too. They can "hurt" in the moment, but friend, think of life's changes as growing pains. They can be a good thing. That's because God is working in and through all things—not only for us but for everyone else too.

Embrace Your New

If you're struggling with change, remember that it's not about you–it's about God. He may make moves so that your job changes to another state or your life takes a new path, but friend, grab hold of His hand and let Him lead you. Trust me–it isn't always easy. But if we focus on Him rather than on the situation, with each step we take, we can look back at how far we've come and see how He's working it all out for His plan.

Nº. 66

RESTORING WHAT WAS LOST

Then he said to the man, "Stretch out your hand."
And the man stretched it out,
and it was restored, healthy like the other.
MATTHEW 12:13

Maybe you picked up this book because you're looking for restoration from something you lost . . . maybe it's time, health, love, a relationship, purpose, hope, identity, peace, or joy. Did you lose time by chasing the wrong things, by putting off what truly mattered, or by being caught up in regrets over past mistakes? Did you lose your health by pushing yourself too hard? Did you lose out on love by being afraid to open your heart? Looking back, we all have regrets. We all wish we could go back in time and get a redo on something. But the truth is, restoration isn't about going back to the way things were. It's about embracing your new, with a deeper understanding of who you are, who God is, and how He desires to heal and renew every part of you.

Think about it this way: Maybe you are who you are today because of what you lost out on in your past. It's easy to carry a lot of hurt and pain, wishing things had been different. But loss does have a way of refining us, of stripping away the things that don't matter, and of making space for something better.

The truth is, we need to accept healing, accept our past, and accept ourselves for who we are—then choose to love ourselves. Today, accept the truth that God loves you. You have the choice today to let go of whatever you are holding on to that you have lost, and to step forward into a bright new future.

Embrace Your New

Today, speak truth to whatever it is that you lost out on. Turn your focus toward God, and ask Him to fill you with peace. You may never understand some things, and that's okay. Ask Him to free your mind and soul from all your regrets and past traumas and to show you a glimpse of the great plans He has for you just ahead.

Nº. 67

BEING MADE NEW

So we do not lose heart. Though our outer self is wasting away, our inner self is being renewed day by day. For this light momentary affliction is preparing for us an eternal weight of glory beyond all comparison, as we look not to the things that are seen but to the things that are unseen. For the things that are seen are transient, but the things that are unseen are eternal.

II CORINTHIANS 4:16–18

Restoration can be painful while the healing is taking place. Sometimes it gets worse before it gets better. I still picture that dresser being stripped of the old paint. Have you ever ripped off a bandage or taped off a wound? It hurts—bad! More tears may be shed during this time than during the initial injury, and the enemy will want you to give up. But friend, try to look through the temporary pain to the "eternal weight of glory."

The restoration process can be painful; it can bring up old memories we don't want to acknowledge; it can bring up mistakes and losses that we don't want to own; and for a while, it can even feel like we are being weighed down with every step we take. As we learned in previous devotions, we can look forward to God making us into a new creation on earth. But we can also look forward to spending eternity in heaven. Having a long-term perspective will help you take your focus off the temporary struggles you face today and put your gaze on the unshakable hope of eternal glory—of the overwhelming joy and perfection that will come in your eternity spent with God. While your inner self is being renewed each day, remember to keep your eyes set on the joy and beauty of God's future kingdom.

Embrace Your New

Friend, can you embrace your new? *Can you allow that old paint to come off? It may be painful to remove, but the end result will be worth it. Digging up old dirt from the past, or leaving it be and covering it with the peace and love that come from God, is a choice—and it's also a gift. Being made new is not an easy process, but hang in there. Set your eternal perspective, and then keep going! Trust me, it's* worth *it.*

Nº. 68

NOT FEELING LOVED

But God shows his love for us
in that while we were still sinners,
Christ died for us.
ROMANS 5:8

Do you ever feel unloved by the people who are supposed to be in your inner circle? You've been open and honest about how they make you feel, and you've even helped them understand ways to show their love for you—and yet nothing changes. The feeling of being "unloved" can lead to loneliness, depression, and even anger. But what can we do? We can't make others love us. Romans 12:9 says, "Let love be genuine. Abhor what is evil; hold fast to what is good." So, even when we feel hurt and disappointed, we are called to respond with love that is genuine, not fake or shallow. Instead of responding out of bitterness or pretending everything is fine when it's not, we should respond by reflecting God's sincere love. This could look like having difficult but honest conversations, seeking reconciliation, or asking forgiveness.

Are you holding on to any bitterness toward God? Somewhere deep down, you might be wondering why He didn't come through for you. And this one little thought could make you question His love for you as well. Sometimes we need to restore our view of how much God loves us. First John 4:8 reminds us that God is love. He loves you so much that He calls you a masterpiece. He loves you so much that He longs to be your Redeemer, your Savior, your Restorer. God's love is everlasting. He knows you—inside and out. He knows your thoughts, your actions, and your heart, and He loves you unconditionally. There is *nothing* that can ever separate His love from you, no matter what.

Embrace Your New

Jeremiah 31:3–4 (THE MESSAGE) says, "I've never quit loving you and never will. Expect love, love, and more love! And so now I'll start over with you and build you up again." The Lord is pursuing you, and I hope you run to Him for refuge as your faith in Him strengthens, no matter the season. I pray that you will always find the truest love in Him.

N°. 69

TRUST IN OTHERS

Put not your trust in princes,
in a son of man, in whom there is no salvation.
When his breath departs, he returns to the earth;
on that very day his plans perish. Blessed is he whose help
is the God of Jacob, whose hope is in the Lord his God.

PSALM 146:3-5

When we trust people, they can sometimes leave us broken and upset. It is so good to know that even when people disappoint us, we can put our trust in God. We know that things of this earth can fail, crumble, fall apart, and sink into the depths of the sea—but Jesus and His love for us last forever.

While it is important to build community and build trust with your spouse, family, and friends, Psalm 146:3 tells us not to place our ultimate trust in other humans (even those with high status). Not one person on this earth, no matter who they are, can provide ultimate security or salvation. Their power is limited, and they are subject to the same frailties as everyone else. But God's power is unlimited, and His plans endure forever. If you are putting your ultimate trust in your dad or your spouse or any human being, you are going to be disappointed, because humans are imperfect. True blessing and security come from depending on the Lord, who promises to be your help and hope forever.

Embrace Your New

If you've never read through the book of Psalms, I encourage you to do so on your journey of restoration. This book of the Bible talks about trust—a lot. Let's end today with some truths from Psalms (and one verse from Proverbs). Psalm 56:3–4 says: "When I am afraid, I put my trust in you. In God, whose word I praise, in God I trust; I shall not be afraid. What can flesh do to me?" Proverbs 3:5 reminds us: "Trust in the LORD with all your heart, and do not lean on your own understanding." And Psalm 118:8 says: "It is better to take refuge in the LORD than to trust in man." Friend, take refuge in God today and allow Him to work in and through you as you trust Him along your path to restoration.

N°. 70

A HEART OF LOVE

"I will give you a new heart,
and a new spirit I will put within you.
And I will remove the heart of stone from your flesh
and give you a heart of flesh."
EZEKIEL 36:26

A "heart of stone" could be described as rebellious and unresponsive. It signifies a lack of compassion or empathy. Some people have a heart of stone because they know God, but they still reject Him. Others develop a heart of stone after suffering abuse, enduring disappointment, or grieving the loss of a loved one. Instead of seeking restoration or healing, they shut down emotionally, allowing their hearts to harden. On the other hand, a "heart of flesh" can be described as soft and tender. It signifies love toward others. Those with a heart of flesh are humble, teachable, and open to God's Word. They practice repentance and forgiveness. So the question is: Which heart do you have? Or are you somewhere in between?

When everything seems to be falling apart, it's easy to start building up walls around your heart because you don't want to get hurt again. You may have done everything God asked you to do, but it led you down a path you didn't want to take. Your friends and family may have abandoned you in your time of need, and now, when you look around, all you see are dark skies and unhappy faces. If this is you, God can restore your heart. He can soften the edges, get rid of all the hurt and resentment, and make your heart new again—so you can love again, feel free again. You will even be able to see the bluebird in the tree and the joy on your neighbor's face. Today, pray that God begins to knock off any stone that has built up on your heart over the years—ask Him to create a pure heart in you. Then open your eyes to all the goodness He has to show you.

Embrace Your New

We often think that if we are hurt by someone, then everyone else will hurt us too, and this can prevent us from having healthy relationships. Friend, today I want to bring you the good news that God can soften these hard feelings in your heart, no matter how they came to be.

As the heavens are higher than the earth, so are my ways higher than your ways.

Isaiah 55:9

Nº. 71

YOU ARE WHO . . .

Therefore, if anyone is in Christ,
he is a new creation.
The old has passed away;
behold, the new has come.
II CORINTHIANS 5:17

We know that generational issues can stay with us, and then be passed on to the next generation. In order for this cycle to stop, it takes one person who steps off the hamster wheel, looks around, and decides, *It ends with me*. Friend, I am that person for my family, and that's why I'm standing here on my soapbox telling you that you can be that person too!

Often, we don't see all the hidden pains that lie within us or understand why we are the way we are until God helps us to uncover the reasons. But God can wipe away generational trauma, pain, and anything you carry—even things that hurt others too. You can decide to be the one in your family to stop this cycle, not allowing this pain to continue with your children and then their children. You can do the hard work along with God, as painful as it is, to be freed of things that may seem normal but aren't. You can be filled instead with God's peace, love, grace, and understanding. You can do this even if you're afraid. You can do this even if you're unsure. You can do this with the strength from the Holy Spirit, who lives within you as a believer in Christ. You can cling to that strength as the tides get strong and you start to shed what has been within you for so long. You can begin to accept a new you—a new life that is found in Christ, your Redeemer!

Embrace Your New

Today's devotion might be hard. Everyone's story is different, and we can grow so used to things that we think we're just fine when we're not. If we take a look inside ourselves and really see what plagues our hearts–anxieties, worries, the ways we treat others, how we think of the world–we will realize that we all are broken and need Jesus. If you feel like you have experienced trauma in the past, or you're in a place where you are ready to stand up and say, "It ends with me," think about seeing a professional counselor to help you in this restoration process.

N°. 72

JESUS OVER EVERYTHING

"For my thoughts are not your thoughts,
neither are your ways my ways, declares the Lord.
For as the heavens are higher than the earth,
so are my ways higher than your ways and
my thoughts than your thoughts."

ISAIAH 55:8-9

During this season of embracing your new, it's imperative for you to remember that God's perspective on your life is infinitely broader and wiser than your own. His thoughts and ways are beyond anything we could ever fully understand. It may be that you were going along perfectly in this process, learning to surrender and notice His nudges, and then all of a sudden you got hit with something out of left field—something you didn't see coming. Please know that this was not out of the blue for God. *He* saw it coming. And this something you got hit with—how does it feel? Is it a new job that matches your skill set? Is it a new opportunity that seems way out of your wheelhouse? Is it the start of a new relationship? It sounds like you have some decisions to make.

The key to fully embracing your new is to keep Jesus at the center—over everything. He holds all the answers. Jesus will guide you in the right direction, and He will calm your anxieties and fears. Remember, Jesus invites us to a life of abundant renewal, not bound by our limited understanding of how things should go. So, if this opportunity seems outrageous, that doesn't mean it's not for you. If you feel that God is opening a door for you, trust Him. His "new" for us is better even than our own ideas. Chances are, Jesus is calling you into something greater, something bigger, than you can imagine. Are you ready for the profound transformation that God has in store for you?

Embrace Your New

Give God the glory. From Him are all things, and to Him are all things. Accept today the gift that is Jesus. Accept the love and peace that is freely given and available to you. Surrender it all to Him, and trust and believe in Him. Remember, Jesus is over everything.

N°. 73

YOUR GIFTS

As each has received a gift,
use it to serve one another,
as good stewards of God's varied grace.
I PETER 4:10

Having gifts that differ
according to the grace given to us,
let us use them.
ROMANS 12:6

God has uniquely equipped you with gifts. And there's is no better feeling than when you know your life is aligned with God's plan for you. That's when you get to use your gifts—gifts crafted specifically for you—and share them with the world. When you find yourself in this place, you might have the urge to overinflate your self-worth, forgetting who placed you in that position. But it's important to give God the glory, knowing that everything you have is from Jesus. You may find that your new position causes you to feel insecure and uncertain. In this case, remember that God's plan for you will prevail, so lean into Him for strength and courage. He isn't looking for perfection—He is only looking for surrender and obedience. So just take the next step.

Also, letting others know where you are at in your personal restoration story with God can play a vital role in someone else's life. You don't have to wait to share what God is doing in your life until you feel as if the process is complete. Share your story today—and don't leave out the hard parts. It's important to be vulnerable with those you trust so they will feel open to ask questions and learn more. Speak the truth in love. Be fully who God created you to be! You could change the trajectory of someone's life today without even knowing it.

Embrace Your New

Embracing your new self may mean that you feel a little unsteady at first. It may feel like you're walking for the first time. But keep taking that next step toward surrender, toward obedience—all the while making sure you're in step with Him. God has given you so many gifts to share with the world, and He has so many wonderful plans for how you can do that. Embrace your unique place in this world today, and look with a grateful heart to others whom He has called to embrace their unique places in this world as well.

N°. 74

RELEASING YOUR PAST

Jesus said to him,
"No one who puts his hand to the plow and looks back is fit for the kingdom of God."
LUKE 9:62

Think back to that dresser we've been talking about . . . how it was so broken and joyless, faded and damaged from years of living in this imperfect world. It had scratches, dings, cracks, and rust covering its exterior. And it was cast away, discarded as if it was a lost cause, before Jesus carried it into His workshop. Friend, we may always remember the scratches, dings, and cracks of our lives, even after we've been restored. Those times in our lives that hurt so bad that they left a mark on our souls will not simply go away without a trace. They will always be a part of our story; the trick is not allowing them to define us.

Isaiah 43:18 reminds us: "Remember not the former things, nor consider the things of old." Choosing to dwell in the pain of your past can stall your restoration process. It's perfectly okay to feel your feelings toward a certain situation or person. Take time to get to the root of those emotions, allow yourself time and space to truly experience them, and let the feelings run their course. But God doesn't want you to hold on to your hurt or your anger or your suffering forever. He wants to fill in the cracks, strip off the paint, and sand down the hurt that has held you captive. The question is: Are you ready to release it? Or do you wear your pain as a badge? In your heart of hearts, are you a little afraid that if you let it go, the person who harmed you will not get their due? Or that if you forget it, the world wouldn't have to pay for it? Friend, ask yourself this: *How freeing would it be to lay it all down and walk away?*

Embrace Your New

What past pain are you trying to ignore? Did you know it's better to deal with your emotions than to try to push them to the side? Ask Jesus to be with you today as you experience the disappointment, fear, anger, or frustration that comes from that past pain. Only then can you truly release it and be present—ready to move forward in the process.

Nº. 75

HEALING

Heal me, O Lord,
and I shall be healed;
save me, and I shall be saved,
for you are my praise.
JEREMIAH 17:14

Our God is a God of healing. We often think of physical healing when we hear that word, but we can also be spiritually healed or emotionally healed . . . there are all kinds of ways we're able to be made new. Our God is a God of miracles—and yes, they still happen today!

If you are in need of healing—no matter if it is a healing of the mind, body, or soul—you can pray. Mark 11:24 reminds us: "Therefore I tell you, whatever you ask in prayer, believe that you have received it, and it will be yours." Let this verse be an invitation to trust that God sees your struggle, understands your pain, and holds your future in His hands. Know that God is not only able to heal you, but He desires to heal you. And while God may not heal you in the time or manner in which you would prefer, you can rest in the knowledge that God doesn't just mend; He redeems.

The healing process—whether spiritual, physical, or

emotional—often takes longer than we expect. It's important to take one day at a time, and to celebrate even the smallest wins along the journey. Have you started to see a past hurt from a different, more hopeful angle? That's so great! Are you starting to have the desire to forgive someone? Wonderful! Have you been able to get more sleep lately? That's amazing! Do you feel even a tad bit stronger when it comes to your spiritual, physical, or emotional life? That is truly fantastic! No victory is too small to celebrate. Remember, God's restoration is not just about healing wounds—it's about making you whole in ways you never imagined. There's no doubt that on the other side of this, you'll know it was worth the wait.

Embrace Your New

Pray this prayer right now: Lord, I come to You today to ask for healing. You know what needs to be mended in my life even more than I do. I place my healing in Your hands. I trust You, Lord, to take my life and make something beautiful out of my brokenness. In Jesus' name, amen.

Nº. 76

CLEANSING FROM SIN

But your iniquities have made
a separation between you and your God,
and your sins have hidden his face
from you so that he does not hear.
ISAIAH 59:2

Today's verse tells us that at times, our sins can keep us from connecting with God. Isaiah 59:2 refers to a time when the spiritual condition of the people of Israel was in a moral decline. During this time, the Bible says there was violence, deceit, idolatry, and hypocrisy. The poor and vulnerable were being exploited, and the leaders and judges were engaged in lies and deception. On top of that, there was an unwillingness to repent. Their sins created a barrier between the people and God, making it impossible for them to experience His presence.

Do you feel like there is a barrier between you and God? Is there sin in your life that needs to be addressed? Remember, a *sin* is defined as any thought, word, action, or behavior that goes against God's will, His commands, or His nature. In many ways, sin can be more about the condition of your heart than it is about your actions, such as having an inward inclination toward pride, anger, selfishness, and wrongdoing. So, while you may not be in a "moral decline," like the Israelites were, could it be that that little piece of rebellion that you're holding on to in your heart is actually creating a barrier in your relationship with God?

You can take refuge in the words of I John 1:9: "If we confess our sins, he is faithful and just to forgive us our sins and to cleanse us from all unrighteousness." Your sins will be completely forgiven today, and any lost connection will be reestablished—if you just ask. What are you waiting for?

Embrace Your New

Jesus died for your sins, my friend. And if you confess those sins and repent, He will forgive you, cleansing your soul and removing any need for shame or guilt. So, why do we still find it difficult to let go of that one little smidge of rebellion? Is it because we feel that if we give it to God, we could lose a part of ourselves? God knows who you are, friend. Decide to go all-in today and give your whole heart to Him. God can take your rebellious heart and give you rest if you allow Him to cleanse your heart by accepting His amazing gift of grace.

N°. 77

RESTORING US TO HIM

Restore us to yourself, O Lord,
that we may be restored!
Renew our days as of old.
LAMENTATIONS 5:21

Let's take a closer look at the word *restored*. In many cases, this word means to bring something back to its original state, or to return to a previous role, or to go back to a previous era or period of time. It's important to understand that when you go through the restoration process with God, it doesn't necessarily mean you are going back to the way things were before. You are being made new. You are entering a new era. This could bring a new way to think, new roles, new positions—a new life. Longing for the past is a natural part of the restoration process. We all relate to moments when we look back with nostalgia, wishing for the days when life seemed easier, or when we felt closer to God.

For what parts of your past are you longing today? Have you given yourself permission to acknowledge the pain of that loss? Today, take your pain to God, and lean into your relationship with Him. As it is restored, you will grow to trust Him more and more. Being close to Him doesn't mean that all your desires will be met, but rather that your heart will be *in tune* with His so that His desires for you will be met and He will restore you to Him. The days of old may have been good, but the future that God is *preparing* for you will be even better.

Embrace Your New

Take a heart check today, friend, and think about what you are expecting to get out of this process. Have you asked God whether your anticipated end result is aligned with His? Ultimately, the greatest thing we can expect from God's restorative work is a deeper relationship with Him, an increased awareness of His love, and the transformation of our hearts. So, while you may never go back to the way things were, or if doors with new opportunities haven't opened for you yet, or if you are still grieving the tragedy of your loss, know that God is doing something new, whether you see it or not. You are growing stronger, wiser, and more resilient. Hang in there, my friend. He is working!

N°. 78

DANCING IN THE RAIN

Jesus wept.

JOHN 11:35

It was raining the other day, and my daughter wanted to play outside. I told her, "Well, it's raining . . ." and she said, "I don't care." She went inside, put on her rain boots, grabbed her umbrella, and then headed outdoors to dance in the rain and jump in the puddles. We all need to take note of how children see the world rather than just looking at it through an adult lens. The adult would likely think, *It's raining—there's no way to have any fun in the rain! We have to take shelter indoors.* But children, like my daughter, challenge that and see beauty, fun, and opportunity—even in the rain.

Do you know what's great about the rain? It refreshes the earth and allows for trees, plants, and flowers to grow. Have you ever thought of your tears as internal rainstorms? Just as rainstorms build up and then burst, releasing an outpouring of water, emotions often accumulate inside us until they overwhelm us and need to be released. Tears allow all our pent-up feelings to pour out in a way that leaves us feeling relieved, refreshed, and cleansed.

Don't be afraid of crying during this process, friend. Let that internal rainstorm burst! Our tears can lead to growth. Find peace in knowing Jesus cried too. John 11:35 says that "Jesus wept." Friend, He understands—He's been there! He has experienced the same kind of deep sorrow that we have. Rely on God, allowing Him to take whatever burdens you carry. When you do, He will hold you in your pain. And you'll come to know that with God holding you, you can withstand any storm, because you are rooted in Jesus Christ—your Savior, your foundation, and your hope!

Embrace Your New

The next time it rains, step out into the storm and feel the raindrops fall upon you. Be reminded that Jesus cried too. Despite the tears, we can be made new in the storms of life! Don't let rain or tears scare you–God is working in and through them. You can dance in the rain!

N°. 79

BEING RIGHT

But I say, walk by the Spirit,
and you will not gratify the desires of the flesh.
GALATIANS 5:16

Do you tend to think you're right most of the time? I'll be honest—I often feel this way. Is it hard to accept that there are other ideas out there, other perspectives that *are* right? As we are being made new, it's important to strip away the belief that we are always right. Instead, what if we opened ourselves up to listening to other people, considered their opinions, and walked in the Spirit rather than in the flesh?

When it's other people's ideas versus ours, demanding to be right can be motivated by something deep inside of us that seeks validation. We want to "win" the argument and have the final word. Is this you? If so, it's important to figure out what that "something deep inside" is. It could be insecurity, fear, or even pride. To walk in the Spirit, you need to choose a different path—one that pursues humility, patience, and peace.

When it's God's Word versus ours, there is no contest. God's Word always wins. Many times throughout the Bible, we are reminded that we don't have all the answers because we cannot see what God sees. Romans 11:33 (NIV) says, "Oh, the depth of the riches of the wisdom and knowledge of God! How unsearchable His judgments, and His paths beyond tracing out!" In Isaiah 55:9 (NIV), God reminds us, "As the heavens are higher than the earth, so are My ways higher than your ways and My thoughts than your thoughts."

As part of your restoration process, God may be asking you to lay down your need to be right all the time. True restoration comes when we surrender our pride and allow God's peace to rule in our hearts, giving us the strength to respond in a way that reflects His love.

Embrace Your New

How many times has "being right" clouded your relationships with others or with God? Maybe it's time to ask God to help you release your need for control. Ask Him to help you respond with understanding and patience, especially in those moments when you feel the urge to defend your ideas or your way of thinking. After all, the restoration process is about healing, not winning.

Nº. 80

FEELING BAD ABOUT...

I praise you,
for I am fearfully and wonderfully made.
Wonderful are your works;
my soul knows it very well.
PSALM 139:14

Please always remember this: You are fearfully and wonderfully made. You were created by God—and that's a beautiful thing. It's easy to be hard on yourself, feel bad about things, and bring yourself down. Even when you do things for *you*, you may feel bad about that (guilty here!). I'm here to tell you that you deserve to do some things for you. Do you feel bad daily about each decision you make, questioning your every step and wondering how you could have made a better decision? Try not to overthink it, my friend. You likely made the best decision for you at the time. You are here, on this planet, at this time in history, for a reason. God made your mind. He knew what decision you would make before anyone posed the question. God wants you to live and be in this world just as you. Now, do you ever feel bad about making the choices that God called you to make? Stop there, friend. Don't feel guilty about leaving a place that God wants you to leave. Remember, don't look back! Keep your focus on Him and let Him lead you onward to what's next.

Sometimes you may feel like you're a burden to others when you're the one who needs help. Friend, you aren't a burden. I, too, have been there—I even said "sorry" to the nurses in the delivery room when I was giving birth! But remember—you were fearfully and wonderfully made by God, and you are not a burden. Even if others have made you feel that way in the past, that's something they need to work on—it has nothing to do with you. You don't need to feel bad about your past or your present, for you are a child of God!

Embrace Your New

The next time you put yourself down, thinking you aren't worthy of others' time or help, instead tell yourself, I am worthy. *You are more than those negative thoughts that make you believe you are not valuable. Don't let evil win out–replace those negative thoughts with truth whenever they enter your mind. You don't have to feel bad about anything if you are truly seeking to please the Lord in all that you do.*

Delight yourself in the LORD, and he will give you the desires of your heart.

Psalm 37:4

N°. 81

LIVE YOUR LIFE

"The thief comes only
to steal and kill and destroy.
I came that they may have life
and have it abundantly."
JOHN 10:10

We've all heard that voice in our heads saying, *You'll never amount to anything. You'll always be sad. You won't find joy in anything. You aren't worthy of happiness . . .* The negativity can go on and on. Evil is the thief that comes to destroy us, friend. And the sad part is, we often believe these lies over what God thinks of us. We think, *I can't be restored—I have to remain sad. I don't deserve love or happiness. My relationships always fail . . . No one wants to be my friend . . .* Friend, stop these thoughts in their tracks! Replace all those negative thoughts in your head with words of truth: you are God's handiwork, created in Christ Jesus to do good works (Ephesians 2:10); you are precious and honored in His sight (Isaiah 43:4); He takes great delight in you, and He rejoices over you with singing (Zephaniah 3:17).

Jesus came so that you "may have life, and have it to the full" (John 10:10 NIV). What does it mean to live your life in the fullest sense? While it does mean you don't have to listen to the lies that say you are broken beyond repair, it also means you can live free of shame, regret, and all your past failures. He wants you to live an abundant life, knowing that you are here on purpose, for a purpose. He wants you to embrace His peace and joy. You are not here just to survive—you are here to thrive, to live life to the fullest, and to enjoy His creation. So yes, release the lies of the thief who came to steal, but also grab hold of the abundant life that God is offering you.

Embrace Your New

What is keeping you from living your life freely and abundantly? As you start to find yourself thinking negative thoughts, write them down, then beside those words, write a Scripture that reminds you of the truth. You were not created to live in the shadows of your brokenness but to live in the light of deep joy—the kind that comes from knowing you are loved, accepted, and secure in Jesus.

Nº. 82

OWN WAY VERSUS GOD'S WAY

The heart of man plans his way,
but the Lord establishes his steps.

PROVERBS 16:9

It's easy to feel the tension between our own plans and God's plans, especially when we think we can fix things on our own or we want to rush the restoration process. Sometimes we surrender parts of our lives to God, but we hold on to other areas because we're pretty sure we can handle them on our own. But think about it: Every time you've done it your way, has it ever worked out for you? Even when you mean well, your plans can lead you into the wrong relationship, put you in further financial debt, or lock you into a job you hate.

Psalm 37:4–6 says: "Delight yourself in the Lord, and he will give you the desires of your heart. Commit your way to the Lord; trust in him, and he will act. He will bring forth your righteousness as the light, and your justice as the noonday." So fight the feeling to make a move before asking

God for His guidance or considering whether it aligns with His will. James 4:13–15 (NIV) says: "Now listen, you who say, 'Today or tomorrow we will go to this or that city, spend a year there, carry on business and make money.' Why, you do not even know what will happen tomorrow. What is your life? You are a mist that appears for a little while and then vanishes. Instead, you ought to say, 'If it is the Lord's will, we will live and do this or that.'" It makes sense, right? Why would we move forward with our plans without asking God about them? He is all-knowing, and He only wants the best for us. The next time you're making plans, ask for God's guidance and wisdom, knowing that His plans are much better than anything we could imagine for ourselves.

Embrace Your New

Let's pray: Lord, establish my steps as I lean on You and trust where You are leading me. Help me not to question but just to go where You want me to go, and reassure me along the way that You are leading me. Help me not to want to go my own way but instead to go the way You have established. I trust in You. In Jesus' name, amen.

N°. 83

WEEDS

The Lord is good, a stronghold in the day of trouble;
he knows those who take refuge in him.
NAHUM 1:7

Have you ever spent time pulling weeds? Some weeds have really large thorns. Others are grounded so deep that they leave behind roots, which eventually grow another weed. Weeds have a way of popping up and taking over your garden, flourishing and growing even when the flowers you planted are struggling.

Today, let's think about the weeds in your "soul garden." What weeds are there that you see and think, *I'll get to those later . . .* ? Maybe you have weeds that you've tried to pull out, yet they keep growing back. Or they spread so quickly that now you have tons of other weeds just like them that keep popping up. As you are becoming restored, this is a great time to do some weed pulling. Learn to replace the weeds you don't want in your life with truth and love. Pull out what's no longer serving you—whether it's a relationship, a job, or even hurt from the past. Allow that space to be filled back in with God's love for you and the truth. Allow His peace to come over you as you do the hard work of pulling weeds. You won't always be able to get every weed out, and that's okay. It's a process. Just like we tend to our yards and gardens physically, we need to tend to our hearts, minds, and souls. Pull out the lies you've believed about yourself, others, and God. Pull out the negative self-talk. Pull out the sins you've been hiding away . . . and ask for forgiveness. Then allow God to plant beautiful things in their place.

Embrace Your New

Whether you write it down or just make a list in your mind, decide what you need to pull out of your soul, whether it be unforgiveness, pride, fear, bitterness, or jealousy. If those weeds keep resurfacing, it may be time to address the root cause, dig deeper, and identify the underlying beliefs or wounds that are allowing them to thrive. This could be hard work, but remember: God is with you, empowering you to identify, uproot, and replace the unhealthy things in your life with His love.

Nº. 84

CLEANSE THE HEART

Draw near to God, and he will draw near to you. Cleanse your hands, you sinners, and purify your hearts, you double-minded.

JAMES 4:8

While we're doing the hard work of pulling out weeds, let's also take time to purify our hearts. Sometimes we think there is no way our hearts could ever be "pure" after what we've done in the past. But the truth is, God can create a clean heart within us. James 4:8 tells us that the first step in the purification process is to draw near to God. Spend time with Him through prayer, worship, and Bible reading—make a genuine connection with your Creator. He longs for a relationship with you. The second step is to "cleanse your hands," meaning to confess and repent. Honestly acknowledge areas of sin and bitterness and turn away from those things. Allow God to search your heart and reveal any hidden weeds that need to be healed. The third step is to address the inner conflict of being "double-minded," meaning to have a heart that is divided between trusting God and holding on to your own ways. Do you want God's help, but you are struggling to surrender fully? Part of the purification process is to wholeheartedly trust God and allow Him to guide you.

What do you struggle with most in your faith walk? Do you ask for forgiveness but then fall right back into old sinful patterns? Are you fake toward others? Do you tear yourself down? Friend, even if you find yourself repeating the same sin over and over, continue to talk to God about all of it. He wants to hear it from you. Purification doesn't happen overnight—it's a process that takes time and constant surrender. It's okay to ask for a redo. When we draw nearer and nearer to God with a humble, open heart, He meets us there and cleanses us from the inside out.

Embrace Your New

All our hearts need to be cleansed, friend. Don't worry–you aren't alone! Put it all out there, because God already knows it anyway! Psalm 51:7 says: "Purge me with hyssop, and I shall be clean; wash me, and I shall be whiter than snow." And I John 3:3 gives us this beautiful reminder: "Everyone who thus hopes in him purifies himself as he is pure."

No. 85

ACCEPTING PEACE

Now may the Lord of peace himself
give you peace at all times in every way.
The LORD be with you all.
II THESSALONIANS 3:16

Peace can often feel elusive. The process of restoration isn't quick or easy. And the journey of "embracing your new" can sometimes bring overwhelming feelings of doubt, fear, frustration, and so many more emotions. At times, the highs and lows can make you feel like you're on a roller coaster. One minute you are at peace with your decision, absolutely certain you are aligned with God's will, and you feel closer to Him than ever before. Then the very next minute, you're wondering what you were thinking, questioning whether God actually gave you the green light, and you feel like maybe you didn't hear Him correctly. It can be a lot. When you start to lose your footing and the doubts start to set in, close your eyes and accept God's peace.

Accepting God's peace is part of the restoration process. It doesn't mean that we ignore our struggles or pretend that everything is okay. No, accepting God's peace means we can surrender our doubts, fears, and anxieties into His capable hands. It means that when our minds start racing with all the what-ifs in life, we can open our hearts to God's presence and allow Him to soothe our hearts, minds, and souls. The best part is that we don't have to wait for all the pieces of our lives to be perfectly aligned before we accept His peace. It is not contingent on our circumstances; it is a promise from Him to us. Philippians 4:6–7 (NIV) says, "Do not be anxious about anything, but in every situation, by prayer and petition, with thanksgiving, present your requests to God. And the peace of God, which transcends all understanding, will guard your hearts and your minds in Christ Jesus." Experience His gift of peace today.

Embrace Your New

Friend, I pray today that you will give it all to God and allow Him to come into your heart and life, making your paths straight and calming your soul so you can receive the peace that only comes from Him.

Nº. 86

STOP THE CYCLE

Therefore, as one trespass
led to condemnation for all men,
so one act of righteousness
leads to justification and life for all men.
For as by the one man's disobedience
the many were made sinners,
so by the one man's obedience
the many will be made righteous.

ROMANS 5:18-19

As humans, we are affected by who we are in our DNA and also how we've learned to behave from our parents and those whom we grew up around. Sometimes we don't realize how much our past has shaped us. Many of our social behaviors—such as conflict resolution, manners, and coping mechanisms—are learned behaviors from childhood. As we become adults, we can work to change these behaviors to break the cycle and become better people for ourselves, our children, and everyone around us.

Taking time to consider your childhood—the parent-child relationship, how discipline was handled, how emotions were expressed—can bring light to why you act the way you do. Do you have any learned behaviors that need to be left in the past? Did you feel love from your primary caregiver, or did you feel criticized? Our early relationships with caregivers can shape our relationships as adults. Were you encouraged to pursue your interests as a child, or were you made to feel you weren't good enough? The answer could be affecting your self-esteem as an adult. The good news is that you are able to make decisions today to change your way of thinking, help future generations as well as those around you, and live in the peace that only Jesus can give. We can choose to overcome our unhealthy learned behaviors. We can stop the cycle of negative thoughts and actions and begin something positive and new.

Embrace Your New

Once light has been shed on areas in your life that need to be addressed, you can *change. Therapists are great for giving you the tools to break bad behaviors that stem from your childhood. And you can always lean into God's peace and strength, knowing that He wants you to live abundantly, free from any learned behaviors that are holding you back or could affect the next generation.*

Nº. 87

BE TRANSFORMED

I appeal to you therefore, brothers,
by the mercies of God, to present your bodies
as a living sacrifice, holy and acceptable to God,
which is your spiritual worship.
Do not be conformed to this world,
but be transformed by the renewal of your mind,
that by testing you may discern what is the will of God,
what is good and acceptable and perfect.
ROMANS 12:1–2

When I look at my garden, I love to think of how we planted little seeds, and from those seeds, something amazing happened—they turned into green, growing plants that have provided delicious fruit or gorgeous flowers. Friend, in this restoration process, you can change into something beautiful and joyful too. You can plant seeds of new thoughts, beliefs, and intentions in your heart, but you also need to water those seeds by nurturing and cultivating them. You can do this by making a consistent, conscious effort to see the "new you" grow. This could involve taking action or creating a supportive environment. But be patient as God grows these actions into something new and exciting, fresh and beautiful. There may be some days in this process that it doesn't feel like it, but it is happening! Good things often take time to achieve.

Shedding layers and becoming made new isn't easy, and often it takes the tears and pain of learning more about yourself and uncovering things from your past. But know that God made you with the ability to change. Just because you carry wounds from your past doesn't mean you can go back and fix them, but you *can* decide today to change and be restored rather than staying stuck in your old patterns. You can start to emerge from the seed, as you grow toward the light. Remember, friend, with God *all things* are possible!

Embrace Your New

Friend, read Romans 12:1-2 again. Then know—and believe—that you can be transformed by the renewal *of your mind. Certain patterns and ways can be changed as new pathways are created. It takes time and repetition to allow being made new to happen. But with God's help, you can be transformed. You* can *do this!*

N°. 88

LIVING IN THE FLESH

For if you live according to the flesh you will die,
but if by the Spirit you put to death
the deeds of the body, you will live.
ROMANS 8:13

As we approach the end of this devotional, it's important to discuss the final stages of God's restoration process. You may not be in the final stages yet, and that's okay; it's still good for you to know what to expect. There will be moments when you feel the pull of old habits, fears, and desires—the remnants of the "flesh" that once controlled your life. The battle between living in the flesh and living in the Spirit is part of an ongoing work of transformation. It's not uncommon for parts of your past to keep resurfacing—old ways of thinking, reacting, or coping may try to make their way back into your life. Know this: You are no longer ruled by these ways. Even if you slip and fall back into a pattern, you can always—*always*—turn things around and submit your thoughts, actions, and emotions to God. The restoration process isn't about perfection; it's about constant *surrender*.

You may be tempted to start relying on yourself again or seeking satisfaction and security from the things of this world rather than from God. Don't be discouraged by the fight between temptation and surrender. Recognize the temptations for what they are, and speak God's Word to them. Remember, you are not fighting this alone. The Spirit of God is living inside you. The same Spirit that raised Jesus from the dead is the Spirit on whom you can call to make all those tempting thoughts disappear. God's Spirit has the power to put to death the deeds of the flesh so you can embrace your new identity in Christ. Trust the Spirit. Lean on Him. And begin to live abundantly.

Embrace Your New

If you have accepted Jesus, you now have the Holy Spirit dwelling within you. I encourage you to dive into the Word this week and learn more about the Holy Spirit. Call on the Spirit to help you fight the temptation to fill any voids with earthly pleasures, thoughts, and desires. Allow God's peace and love to flow into your heart and fill you up.

Nº. 89

GOODBYE TO YOUR OLD SELF

To put off your old self,
which belongs to your former manner of life
and is corrupt through deceitful desires,
and to be renewed in the spirit of your minds,
and to put on the new self, created after the likeness
of God in true righteousness and holiness.
EPHESIANS 4:22–24

Take a moment to read Colossians chapter 3 right now. Let its words become a part of your anthem—especially verse 10: "Put on the new self, which is being renewed in knowledge after the image of its creator." That's right. Saying goodbye to your old self does not simply involve leaving behind old behaviors or past mistakes or an old season of life (though that is part of it). It's also about putting on the "new self" that God has created you to be. It's time to embrace your transformation! Ephesians 4:23 (NIV) says we are to be "made new in the attitude of your minds." Has the way you view your past, your worth, and your future now been redefined? Has your mindset shifted with the knowledge that in Christ, you are loved, forgiven, accepted, and equipped for a life of purpose?

As you work through the final stages of the restoration process, you'll notice that your thinking has been rewired to fully embrace who you are becoming. And who is that? Well, you are not the person you once were. You are a child of God, made in His image, and equipped by His Spirit to move into this next phase of life with more confidence, strength, and wisdom than you've ever had before.

Embrace Your New

Remember, the goal of your renewal is to become more and more like Jesus. As you put on your new self, your new identity will shine in ways it didn't before. Have you noticed yourself becoming more compassionate, kind, humble, patient, and loving? Have you noticed that you are now quicker to forgive and slower to anger? What has changed about you? If you don't know the answer, ask someone close to you if they've noticed any changes. Remember, the more you stay grounded in God's Word, the more you will reflect His character in your life.

N°. 90

EMBRACING YOUR NEW

I can do all things through him
who strengthens me.
PHILIPPIANS 4:13

Friend, it's time to embrace your new! I can see Jesus putting the finishing touches on the dresser that was brought into His workshop. You arrived with dings and scratches and many layers of paint. Maybe you even had a few broken drawers or missing pieces of hardware. Throughout this book, God has poured out beautiful reminders of how He has been there for you through it all, encouraging you to *trust in Him* as He *restores* you. You may have shed many tears and done a lot of journaling, or maybe you rested in a peaceful state, simply letting Him restore you. You gave Him all the pain, hurt, and brokenness you've been carrying, and He replaced it all with His love. As He looks at you today, you can hear these words from John 14:27: "Peace I leave with you; my peace I give to you. Not as the world gives do I give to you. Let not your hearts be troubled, neither let them be afraid." Rest in this truth, friend.

When your heart becomes troubled and you start to get some dings on your restored self, come back here and be reminded of God's truth. The trials of the world will always be there, but you can stand firm, having been made new in Christ, knowing who you are and whose you are. I'm so proud of how far you've come, friend. Here's to embracing a brand-new you!

Embrace Your New

Take a moment to thank God for all He does for you. Colossians 3:15 reminds us: "And let the peace of Christ rule in your hearts, to which indeed you were called in one body. And be thankful." Let's pray together: Lord, thank You for carrying me, brokenness and all, into Your workshop. Thank You for being so gentle with me, so patient with me, during the restoration process. Thank You for washing away my tears, for taking all that I've been carrying and replacing it with Your love and peace. Help me to rely on You and Your plans for my life rather than my own. Replace my negative thoughts with Your truth. Continue to work within me each day, as I put my trust in You. In Jesus' name I pray, amen.

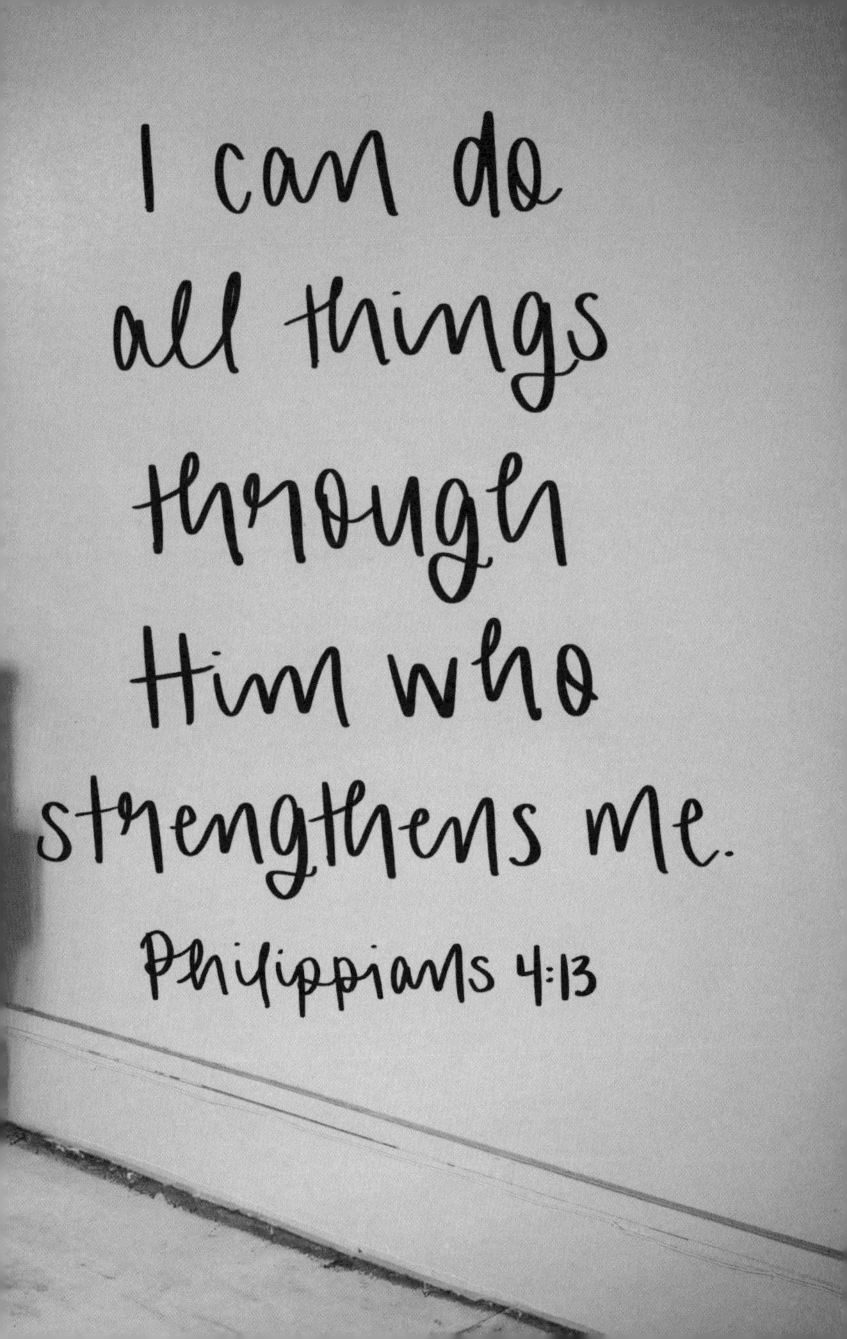

I can do all things through Him who strengthens me.

Philippians 4:13

Dear Friend,

This book was prayerfully crafted with you, the reader, in mind. Every word, every sentence, every page was thoughtfully written, designed, and packaged to encourage you—right where you are this very moment. At DaySpring, our vision is to see every person experience the life-changing message of God's love. So, as we worked through rough drafts, design changes, edits, and details, we prayed for you to deeply experience His unfailing love, indescribable peace, and pure joy. It is our sincere hope that through these Truth-filled pages your heart will be blessed, knowing that God cares about you—your desires and disappointments, your challenges and dreams.

He knows. He cares. He loves you unconditionally.

BLESSINGS!
THE DAYSPRING BOOK TEAM